COUNTERING TRUTH DECAY A RAND Initiative to Restore the Role of Facts and Analysis in Public Life

T0303282

MEDIA LITERACY EDUCATION TO COUNTER TRUTH DECAY

An Implementation and Evaluation Framework

ALICE HUGUET | JOHN F. PANE | GARRETT BAKER
LAURA S. HAMILTON | SUSANNAH FAXON-MILLS

RAND CORPORATION

For more information on this publication, visit **www.rand.org/t/RRA112-18**.

About RAND

The RAND Corporation is a research organization that develops solutions to public policy challenges to help make communities throughout the world safer and more secure, healthier and more prosperous. RAND is nonprofit, nonpartisan, and committed to the public interest. To learn more about RAND, visit www.rand.org.

Research Integrity

Our mission to help improve policy and decisionmaking through research and analysis is enabled through our core values of quality and objectivity and our unwavering commitment to the highest level of integrity and ethical behavior. To help ensure our research and analysis are rigorous, objective, and nonpartisan, we subject our research publications to a robust and exacting quality-assurance process; avoid both the appearance and reality of financial and other conflicts of interest through staff training, project screening, and a policy of mandatory disclosure; and pursue transparency in our research engagements through our commitment to the open publication of our research findings and recommendations, disclosure of the source of funding of published research, and policies to ensure intellectual independence. For more information, visit www.rand.org/about/principles.

RAND's publications do not necessarily reflect the opinions of its research clients and sponsors.

Published by the RAND Corporation, Santa Monica, Calif.

Library of Congress Cataloging-in-Publication Data is available for this publication.

ISBN: 978-1-9774-0663-7

Cover design by Pete Soriano
Cover image: sutthinon602/Adobe Stock.

About This Report

This report is one in a series that is part of the Countering Truth Decay initiative, which is focused on restoring the role of facts, data, and analysis in U.S. political and civil discourse and the policymaking process. The original report, *Truth Decay: An Initial Exploration of the Diminishing Role of Facts and Analysis in American Public Life* (Kavanagh and Rich, 2018) identified a research agenda for studying and developing solutions to the Truth Decay challenge. In July of the following year, the RAND Corporation released a follow-up report linking media literacy to Truth Decay (Alice Huguet, et al., *Exploring Media Literacy Education as a Tool for Mitigating Truth Decay*, 2019). That was followed by several reports in 2020 and 2021:

- Laura S. Hamilton, Julia H. Kaufman, and Lynn Hu, *Media Use and Literacy in Schools: Civic Development in the Era of Truth Decay*, RR-A112-2, 2020a
- Laura S. Hamilton, Julia H. Kaufman, and Lynn Hu, *Preparing Children and Youth for Civic Life in the Era of Truth Decay: Insights from the American Teacher Panel*, RR-A112-6, 2020b
- Alice Huguet, Garrett Baker, Laura S. Hamilton, and John F. Pane, *Media Literacy Standards to Counter Truth Decay*, RR-A112-12, 2021.

This report, the most recent in the series, provides a concise framework of considerations for those implementing ML education (e.g., district decisionmakers, principals, instructional coaches, and teachers) and those evaluating it (e.g., school or district internal evaluators and external evaluators, such as research partners).

RAND Education and Labor

This study was undertaken by RAND Education and Labor, a division of the RAND Corporation that conducts research on early childhood through postsecondary education programs, workforce development, and programs and policies affecting workers, entrepreneurship, and financial literacy and decisionmaking. More information about RAND can be found at www.rand.org. Questions about this report should be directed to ahuguet@rand.org and questions about RAND Education and Labor should be directed to educationandlabor@rand.org.

Funding

Funding for this research is provided by unrestricted gifts from RAND supporters and income from operations.

Acknowledgments

We are grateful to the experts in this field who helped build our understanding of media literacy. Thank you to Michael D. Rich and Jennifer Kavanagh for their guidance, interest, and feedback. We thank LaToya Williams, Fatih Unlu, and Katie Carman for guiding this document through RAND's Research Quality Assurance Process. We are also grateful to Julia Kaufman and Michelle Ciulla Lipkin for comments and insights that undoubtedly improved the report. Any errors are the sole responsibility of the authors.

Summary

In 2021, society continues to face the serious threat of *Truth Decay*, which we describe as the diminishing role that facts, data, and analysis play in our political and civil discourse. Several factors contribute to Truth Decay, including a rapidly evolving information ecosystem and overburdened educational institutions (Kavanagh and Rich, 2018). Many teachers believe that their students lack the complex skills necessary to navigate today's information-saturated world (Hamilton, Kaufman, and Hu, 2020a), and research also demonstrates that this lack of skills is a challenge (Wineburg et al., 2020). This gap—between students' existing competencies and those required for individuals to responsibly and fully engage in a fast-paced media environment—could lead to negative consequences for individuals and society writ large.

The challenge of Truth Decay has led many people to ask what can be done to slow its spread, and media literacy (ML) education has emerged as one promising solution. However, teachers report a lack of guidance around implementing ML education in their practice (Baker, forthcoming), and rigorous research about what kinds of ML education work best (and in what conditions) remains limited. To address these gaps, this report provides a concise framework of considerations for those implementing ML education (e.g., district decisionmakers, principals, instructional coaches, and teachers) and those evaluating it (e.g., school or district internal evaluators and external evaluators, such as research partners).

The chapters of this report focus on each of the six steps in the framework (see Table S.1): (1) identifying ML learning expectations; (2) exploring conditions to support effective implementation; (3) selecting ML learning materials; (4) identifying measures of ML competencies; (5) monitoring interim progress; and (6) measuring summative outcomes. Each chapter highlights how the included information could be useful for implementors of ML programs and evaluators of those programs. In the introductory chapter, we introduce the framework itself and briefly situate it within the broader field of ML, providing an argument for the need for such a tool.

In Chapter Two, we highlight ML standards relevant to Truth Decay, drawing on existing standards from ML and tangential fields (e.g., informa-

TABLE S.1

An Implementation and Evaluation Framework for Media Literacy Education

Phase	Planning for Implementation and Evaluation				Monitoring Implementation	Summative Evaluation
Step	Identifying ML learning expectations	Exploring conditions to support effective implementation	Selecting ML learning materials	Identifying measures of ML competencies	Monitoring interim progress	Measuring summative outcomes

tion literacy, digital literacy). Implementors can adopt or adapt these standards to set ML learning expectations for their students. State policymakers may also be interested in ML implementation when considering how they might integrate ML content on a broad scale. These learning expectations inform the remaining steps in the implementation process, including identifying instructional resources and interim measures of student ML learning. Evaluators can use the standards to align learning expectations, the adopted curriculum, and summative assessments of student learning.

In Chapter Three, we then identify factors in the classroom, school, district, and broader environment that could influence implementation of ML initiatives. This chapter offers implementors a set of planning considerations, and it highlights some important focal points for evaluators collecting implementation data. We focus on three areas that are particularly impactful for educational interventions: establishing a clear vision, building teacher capacity, and providing adequate resources.

In Chapter Four, we define seven dimensions on which ML instructional resources can vary, including such aspects as whether the program is designed to be implemented on its own or integrated into core content-area instruction, how much time it takes, and whether it is intended to be delivered in a particular sequence. Viewing a resource along these dimensions can help educators select instructional resources best suited to their contexts and learning expectations, and also guide any adaptations to those materials they may deem necessary. Evaluators can also use this chapter to inform data collection planning and other aspects of evaluation design.

In Chapter Five, we turn to measurement considerations, including those related to developing or selecting learning assessments, such as alignment to the chosen standards and various other technical features. Educators can use these considerations to assess how well students are learning content and adjust instruction to meet individual- and classroom-level needs. Evaluators will be attuned to selecting an assessment that measures the competencies that the intervention aims to improve and provides evidence that the intervention functions well in populations similar to the population under study.

Having covered these steps related to planning, the report then turns to monitoring implementation of the ML program. For implementors, this includes formative assessment of student learning, gathering qualitative input about student and teacher experiences in the program, and contemplation of factors that are enabling or hindering implementation. Evaluators will want to supplement information about student experience, enablers, and hindrances, including teacher experiences, all with the dual purposes of painting a descriptive picture of implementation and helping to interpret quantitative results on program effects.

Finally, we cover evaluating the impact of ML instruction on student learning, presenting a series of four designs (organized by rigor) and discussing strengths and weaknesses of each in helping implementors understand the success of their initiative. These designs can be accessible to implementors and evaluators because they vary in the degree of required expertise.

To close the report, we remind readers about the urgency of countering Truth Decay, and propose this framework as another step in doing so. We review some of the gaps remaining in ML educational implementation and evaluations. We encourage implementors and evaluators alike to consider this report as a first step and suggest further reading in the included chapters.

Contents

Figures

Tables

CHAPTER ONE

Introduction to the Framework

In 2021, U.S. society faces the continued threat of *Truth Decay*, the diminishing role that facts, data, and analysis play in our political and civil discourse.[1] Several factors contribute to the ubiquity of Truth Decay, including a rapidly evolving information ecosystem and overburdened educational institutions (Kavanagh and Rich, 2018). Many teachers believe that their students lack the complex skills necessary to navigate today's information-saturated world (Hamilton, Kaufman, and Hu, 2020a), and research confirms that this is a challenge (Wineburg et al., 2020). This gap—between students' existing competencies and those required for individuals to responsibly and fully engage in a fast-paced multimedia environment—can lead to negative consequences, such as widespread openness to potentially damaging misinformation, disinformation, and bias. One must only look to the news to see examples of these risks, including such dangers as a lack of reliance on data and facts in the face of conspiracy theories ("Fact Check: No Evidence . . .," 2021) and susceptibility to overseas disinformation campaigns (Tucker, 2020). A heightened awareness of these challenges and their consequences have led many concerned citizens to ask what can be done, and media literacy (ML) education has emerged as one solution with the potential to mitigate the spread of Truth Decay (Huguet et al., 2019).

---

[1] *Truth Decay* is defined by four interrelated trends: an increasing disagreement about objective facts and analytical interpretations of data; a blurring of the line between fact and opinion; an increasing relative volume, and resulting influence, of opinion compared with fact; and declining trust in key sources of information that used to be viewed as sources of factual information, such as the government and the media (Kavanagh and Rich, 2018).

ML is traditionally defined as "the ability to access, analyze, evaluate, create, and act using all forms of communication" (National Association for Media Literacy Education, undated-b). ML addresses the challenges of Truth Decay by focusing on *deconstructing* media messages (e.g., understanding the motivations of an author, analyzing arguments for gaps in logic) and *constructing* media messages (e.g., creating one's own information product). Through ML education, individuals can learn to consume media and contribute to the information ecosystem more responsibly. Importantly, ML teaches students how to think and not *what* to think.

At the time of this report, ML education is not uniformly implemented across the country, across districts, or even throughout schools. ML is not a required core content area in the United States, although an increasing number of states are adding legislation related to ML to their agendas (Media Literacy Now, 2020). Using a nationally representative survey of kindergarten through 12th-grade (K–12) teachers, we know that fewer than one in five schools have adopted explicit ML curricula, and 20 percent of teachers report that their school does not address ML education in any way (Baker, forthcoming). More teachers (40 percent) report integrating ML competencies into existing core content instruction, such as mathematics and language arts, but because most teachers report a lack of school-level directives, this may be happening inconsistently between classrooms.

This scattershot approach to ML education is in part due to (1) a limited understanding about what competencies ML education encompasses, (2) the wide-ranging variety of ML resources available, covering divergent topics, (3) limited rigorous research identifying what kinds of ML education are most effective and under what conditions (Huguet et al., 2019), and (4) the varied ways that ML is outlined in state standards, if it is included at all (Hansen et al., 2018). In this report, we seek to address some of those challenges by outlining a framework for implementing and evaluating ML instruction. We do so by defining ML standards related to Truth Decay, providing a typology to apply to different types of ML resources, and identifying considerations for monitoring implementation and assessing outcomes. We hope this framework reaches educational decisionmakers at multiple levels so that we might begin to see more consistency in ML priorities across schools, districts, and even states.

Given the dual purpose of the framework—to inform both the implementation and evaluation of ML educational efforts—we developed guidance that is relevant to a wide and diverse audience, as illustrated in Table 1.1. The information we provide related to implementation might be of greatest interest to educators, such as classroom teachers. District decisionmakers, principals, instructional coaches, and others who are in close proximity to instruction also fit into our definition of implementors. The other intended audience includes evaluators who are studying the rollout and impact of ML educational interventions. This report should be of particular interest to internal evaluators (e.g., at the school and district levels) who want to better understand the extent to which their ML efforts are successful. This audience may have limited previous exposure to the research strategies that we summarize, and we hope they find value in this report. At the same time, external evaluators—such as researchers who do not work at schools or districts but are interested in conducting evaluations of ML education efforts—might also find parts of this report to be informative for their work. Many researchers conduct evaluations of instructional interventions on a regular basis but lack ML-specific expertise. Therefore, although some of the technical dimensions of this report (e.g., descriptions of randomized controlled trials) will likely be refreshers, we also include information about ML that will likely be new to many evaluators (e.g., the Truth Decay ML standards).

Although two different reports—one for implementors and one for evaluators—would be another approach to reaching these audiences, we believe that the two arenas of practice (the implementors) and research (the

TABLE 1.1

Audience for the Implementation and Evaluation Framework

Implementors	District leaders, principals, instructional coaches, teachers, and others who are in close proximity to instruction.
Evaluators	*Internal evaluators*: Those at the school, district, or state level interested in understanding the extent to which their ML educational efforts are successful, and how to better support ML education. *External evaluators*: Those conducting evaluations, such as researchers, who may be familiar with evaluation methods, but not as familiar with the content of ML education itself.

evaluators) can benefit from greater interaction. Seeing the same chapters through two different lenses can be useful for both parties' purposes; for instance, a district staff member may want to learn how to measure student learning more like an evaluator. Likewise, an evaluator could learn from the implementation factors that implementors consider in their practice. Each chapter of this report closes with considerations for both of these groups.

What We Know About the Effectiveness of ML Education

An important aspect of conceptualizing an ML implementation and evaluation framework is understanding what we currently know about the effectiveness of ML education and interventions.[2] The current state of research on ML effectiveness is generally encouraging, although there are several caveats and important considerations that require further discussion. The following paragraphs provide a simplified "lay of the land" in terms of what we know about ML effectiveness.[3]

ML competencies are difficult to measure well, and the quality and quantity of information and data on the topic are limited. One significant challenge is that interventions and ML education vary widely in scope and population served. Some studies focus on one-off, short-term interventions, while others are embedded into yearlong curriculum. A handful of studies and interventions focus on elementary or middle school-age students, some target high schoolers, and others are aimed at college students. Another challenge is that the concept of ML is defined differently by different orga-

---

[2] Because the work conducted about ML interventions specifically is relatively limited, we include research on closely linked subjects, such as information literacy, digital literacy, and others.

[3] We engaged in an iterative process of reviewing effectiveness studies, using such resources as Education Resource Information Center, Web of Science, and Google Scholar, and such ML websites as the Center for News Literacy (Stony Brook University), the Media Education Lab (University of Rhode Island), and others. We also relied on reference lists from included work and recommendations from colleagues and experts. For a more in-depth literature review and discussion of methodology, see Huguet et al., 2019.

nizations, researchers, and practitioners. These challenges make it difficult to aggregate the limited findings that we do have. An additional obstacle is that nearly all of the studies in the ML field are descriptive or correlational in nature, which can be valuable for learning more about the context of ML but is not sufficient for drawing conclusions about effectiveness. Only a small handful of studies employ basic pre- and postassessments with a treatment and control group, while only one study that we know of employs a causal research design (McGrew et al., 2019). Many studies lack in-depth descriptions of the interventions' implementation, making it difficult to parse exactly what it is that "worked" in the studies.[4] With these limitations in mind, we are still able to make preliminary inferences and discuss what the evidence does suggest.

One recent and particularly rigorous effectiveness study was conducted by McGrew et al., 2019. This study engaged 67 college students enrolled in a critical thinking and writing course, which was a general education requirement for the university. Students were randomly assigned to treatment and control conditions. In this case, the treatment was two 75-minute instructional modules taught by two authors of the study in the middle of the semester. Students' ability to evaluate online sources was assessed at the beginning and end of the semester. The study's results are encouraging, particularly considering the relatively low-lift intervention: Students in the treatment group were 2.15 times more likely to score higher at posttest than pretest; students who had the instructional module made significantly more progress in their ability to evaluate online sources compared with students who did not.

As previously mentioned, the modalities, samples, and methodologies used for evaluating effectiveness vary significantly—which can make it difficult to aggregate evidence. That being said, the remaining studies in our sample have results that mostly mirror the positive findings from McGrew et al., 2019. For instance, using a quasi-experimental design with a large sample of middle school students, Fingar and Jolls, 2014, find evidence that students whose teachers received ML training saw their ML competencies improve compared with a control group. However, that improvement wore

[4] We discuss implementation further in Chapter Three.

off in a second posttest administered after the initial posttest, which suggests that these skills may need to be continually cultivated over time. Hobbs and Frost, 2003, evaluated a yearlong initiative at a high school to convert a language arts course into being more ML-focused. They found that students in this course performed better than a control group of students on several ML-related skills, including deciphering evidence and identifying the purpose of the author. A different study using task-based assessments found that results were mixed—the treatment group outperformed the control group on some tasks but not others. However, the author posits that some tasks may have been too easy, leading to the two groups scoring similarly (Weber, 2012). This finding illuminates the importance of designing valid and reliable measurements and points to a need for better documentation of implementation conditions—both of which are pertinent challenges that we will discuss later in this report.

Framework for Implementing and Evaluating Media Literacy Educational Efforts

Our report is organized around the framework outlined in Table 1.2. This table identifies three phases of implementation and evaluation: planning, monitoring implementation, and assessing the summative impact of the ML educational effort. Each step within these phases comprises one chapter of this report.

The first two framework chapters are foundational to implementing or evaluating any ML educational efforts. Chapter Two introduces learning standards that can help focus ML efforts (e.g., the standards can support selection of learning resources) and inform outcome-related research questions for an evaluation. In Chapter Three, we delve into research about factors that support successful implementation of ML education and related initiatives. That chapter describes different layers of implementation—beginning with the classroom, radiating out to the school, and then to the district and broader environment—each with influence over multiple conditions (e.g., a clear and shared vision for ML instruction) that can affect the effectiveness of ML education efforts. For implementors at every level, this chapter highlights factors to consider when planning for ML instruc-

TABLE 1.2

An Implementation and Evaluation Framework for Media Literacy Education

Phase	Planning for Implementation and Evaluation				Monitoring Implementation	Summative Evaluation
Step	Identifying ML learning expectations	Exploring conditions to support effective implementation	Selecting ML learning materials	Identifying measures of ML competencies	Monitoring interim progress	Measuring summative outcomes
Tools	Truth Decay Media Literacy Standards (Figure 2.1)	Dimensions influencing implementation (Figure 3.1)	Typology of ML resources (Figure 4.1)	List of assessment types and considerations (Table 5.1)	Table of potential monitoring activities (Table 6.1)	Research design types and features (Table 7.1)
Implementation considerations	Use standards to develop a shared vision of ML; inform selection of instructional resources and assessments of student learning	Consider local context, identify needs, advocate for additional support	Adopt, adapt, or create resources that align with instructional needs	Develop or select measures of student learning based on alignment to learning goals, instruction, and resources	Make updates to instruction and policies based on formative assessments and qualitative data	Plan and administer assessments for purpose of understanding "final" learning for course
Evaluation considerations	Use standards to identify measures and define outcome-related questions the evaluation seeks to address	Define questions related to implementation that the evaluation seeks to address, consider methods	Use the typology to identify the best approaches to evaluating an ML intervention	Develop or select measures of evaluating student learning for the purpose of evaluating effectiveness	Monitor formative assessments and implementation conditions for insights, and to identify factors that might explain outcomes	Plan and administer summative evaluation to determine effectiveness of intervention, answer research questions

tion; for instance, if a teacher knows that they will not receive ML training from their school, they might seek a resource that includes such training. For evaluators, this chapter helps to identify areas of focus for data collection, particularly for collecting implementation data.

In Chapter Four, we introduce a taxonomy of ML resources. Given the wide variety of resources available, this taxonomy can help implementors determine the kinds of resources that will meet their needs. The taxonomy is also informative for evaluators because the type of resource provided in an intervention will, to some extent, influence the design of the evaluation. We do not provide guidance about *evaluating* the resources themselves; instead, this chapter should be read as part of the preparation phase, to be considered prior to implementation or evaluation of ML educational efforts.

The next two chapters address issues of measurement and monitoring. Chapter Five explores considerations related to measurement of ML competencies, a particular challenge given their complexity. This chapter can help implementors and evaluators consider the kinds of assessments they should select or develop. In Chapter Six, we explore ways to monitor the implementation of ML education, from conducting interviews and observations to document collection. District decisionmakers, principals, instructional coaches, and teachers might find information on formative assessment (FA) and implementation monitoring useful for adjusting their practice, while evaluators can use this chapter to help identify areas of focus for monitoring progress in implementation. Chapter Seven then addresses quantitative summative evaluation, and how implementors and evaluators can approach assessing the impact of an ML intervention. We close the report with some key takeaways for readers regarding the importance of implementing and monitoring ML in an era of Truth Decay.

The position in which ML finds itself—as a form of education that appears to be effective but is somewhat understudied—supports the need for this report. Because we have some confidence in the effectiveness of ML interventions, it is reasonable for implementors to move forward with ML educational efforts using the implementation framework. However, we still need more-rigorous research, which explains why an evaluation framework is needed.

CHAPTER TWO

Identifying Media Literacy Learning Expectations

Phase	Planning for Implementation and Evaluation				Monitoring Implementation	Summative Evaluation
Step	Identifying ML learning expectations	Exploring conditions to support effective implemen-tation	Selecting ML learning materials	Identifying measures of ML comp-etencies	Monitoring interim progress	Measuring summative outcomes

In this chapter, we share a set of core ML learning expectations that can support implementors, such as districts, schools, and teachers, in determining where they should focus their efforts, and can support evaluators in grounding their data collection and analysis. In Chapter One, we shared a commonly used definition of *media literacy*: "the ability to access, analyze, evaluate, create, and act using all forms of communication" (National Association for Media Literacy Education, undated-b). This definition encompasses a wide array of competencies; for instance, teachers can interpret the term *analyze* to mean many different things. Relatedly, a variety of existing ML resources focus on vastly different skills while still operating under the umbrella of ML, which can make it difficult to select resources to fit specific needs (Huguet et al., 2019). Greater delineation of these competencies is needed to guide educational and measurement activities; we know that most teachers believe that it is important for their students to learn skills related to ML (Hamilton, Kaufman, and Hu, 2020a), but the multitude of available resources can make it difficult to know where to start. Teachers want additional guidance related to what ML entails (Baker et al., forthcoming).

A lack of clarity about the specific competencies that compose ML is not only a problem for those in the classroom. It can also challenge evaluators hoping to understand what kinds of ML education work best and how ML education can be implemented effectively. Extant research about the effectiveness of ML education focuses on various skills, such as understanding that media images are often unrealistic (Fingar and Jolls, 2014), critically evaluating and applying research to problems (Crist, Duncan, and Bianchi, 2017), detecting bias, and interpreting news stories (Tully, Vraga, and Smithson, 2020), among other skills. The wide-ranging interpretations of ML competencies pose challenges in aggregating research on the effectiveness of ML educational interventions.[1]

In this chapter, we briefly describe our effort to address this challenge by developing a set of 15 Truth Decay ML standards.[2] Standards are developed by subject-matter experts, and school districts, states, or other bodies adopt those standards to guide decisions about instruction and assessment. Educational standards typically specify "what students should know and be able to do" (Dusenbury et al., 2020, p. 3) rather than describing pedagogical practices. Standards provide educators with information about learning expectations but do not dictate how educators should go about ensuring that students meet those expectations. Standards can help create a common language about the knowledge, skills, and dispositions that students should master, and they can also serve as a means of communicating expectations about what outcomes educators should prioritize (Collaborative for Academic, Social, and Emotional Learning, undated; Hamilton, Stecher, and Yuan, 2012). Despite the importance of standards, a list of relevant, modern ML standards that are agreed upon across the field does not exist.

In the sections to follow, we briefly describe our methodology for creating the standards and present the standards themselves. We then describe ways that standards are foundational for planning processes undertaken

---

1 The National Association for Media Literacy Education and its partners are undertaking a research initiative to build a common framework for identifying and measuring impactful media literacy practices in the United States (see National Association for Media Literacy Education, undated-a).

2 A more-detailed description of these standards and the methods we used to develop them is provided in a separate report (Huguet et al., 2021).

by implementors and evaluators alike. We emphasize that the standards we offer do not encompass the full array of ML competencies; instead, our selected standards are a synthesized list distilled using the specific lens of Truth Decay.

Developing Truth Decay Media Literacy Standards

We engaged in a systematic, multiphase process to produce the Truth Decay ML standards presented in this report. We reviewed standards related to ML, news literacy, information literacy, digital literacy, and other relevant subject areas. We also examined social and emotional learning (SEL) standards, Common Core State Standards, Next Generation Science Standards, and other standards that overlap with the content of ML—all of which were written by experts in their fields. We sought to narrow these lists exclusively to standards related to Truth Decay and then synthesize those lists into one simplified set. By applying the Truth Decay lens, we excluded competencies that are undoubtedly relevant to participating in the information ecosystem but not to the core of Truth Decay—such as technical skills (e.g., keyboard and mouse skills). We also focused less on creativity in our ML standards than we would have if we were not focused on Truth Decay—for example, we did not include such standards as, "Create multimedia presentations with multiple pages, audio, images, and transitions for individual assignments" (Arizona Department of Education, Educational Technology Division, 2009).[3]

The wording of our Truth Decay ML standards is drawn from other standards that were generally written for the high school level, but we believe these standards can inform instruction at all grade levels. We opted for high school because adolescents' typical cognitive development makes this group particularly well suited for instructional experiences that address the often-complex phenomena related to Truth Decay. At the same time, those who work with younger students might find these standards to be a useful reference for thinking about longer-term ML goals and informing the

---

[3] Greater details on our methods for developing our list, and a full list of the sets of existing standards referenced for this chapter, are provided in Huguet et al., 2021.

creation of developmentally appropriate standards for their students. Given that elementary and middle school students also access media (including the internet)—often without adult supervision—these standards can provide an important starting point for conversations about younger students' ML needs.

Truth Decay Media Literacy Standards

The standards in Figure 2.1 include competencies that are required to engage in the information ecosystem in a way that can help slow Truth Decay. The standards are organized into four categories that align with the four trends of Truth Decay. We do not provide detailed descriptions of each standard or instructional guidance; rather, we identify the primary competencies that implementors can promote to equip their students to limit the spread of Truth Decay and can use to inform their evaluation design.

Although we organized our list of standards using the four trends of Truth Decay, these trends are not mutually exclusive. They are interrelated by their nature; therefore, some standards could fall under more than one trend. We selected one trend for placement of each standard for the purpose of organization, but we encourage readers to consider ways that the standards might cross the boundaries of these categories.

How This Chapter Can Inform the Implementation and Evaluation of Media Literacy Educational Efforts

As already noted, this chapter synthesizes myriad existing standards that specifically address the challenge of Truth Decay to identify a single, concise set. Ideally, standards would be selected at higher levels of the educational system, such as at the state level, rather than being used on a teacher-by-teacher basis (or, for evaluators, a study-by-study basis). However, we provide these standards for the individual reader because, at the time of this report, there is limited action related to ML standards at these higher levels of the U.S. education system (Media Literacy Now, 2020). For instance, few states have adopted standards related to ML, and districts may not be considering ML as an area of focus. Therefore, it may be necessary for implementors and evaluators to familiarize themselves with these standards for their planning purposes.

These Truth Decay ML standards could be useful for district leaders, principals, instructional coaches, and teachers planning ML implementation. For such organizational leaders as district decisionmakers and principals, these standards may help to define their vision around ML—an important factor in implementation, as discussed in Chapter Three. Having common language around instructional concepts can support successful educational efforts—particularly in non-core content areas similar to ML, such as SEL (Oberle et al., 2016)—and standards such as these add more-concrete definitions to instructionally ambiguous terms, such as *analyze* and *evaluate*. Therefore, these standards can be used to inform the vision and common language ideal for implementation.

Teachers and coaches in varied grade levels and subject areas can also use these standards to prepare for implementation. In cases where teachers need to select their own resources to bring ML into their classrooms, these standards can assist in that selection process.[4] In selecting ML activities or curricula, teachers might consider the degree to which their options incorporate the 15 standards identified here; some ML programming might focus on content that—although potentially useful in other ways—does not address or only partially addresses the immediate public threat of Truth Decay. In addition to informing the selection of resources, these standards can help teachers integrate ML into classes for which they already have curriculum. One way to teach ML is through integrating competencies in all subject areas (e.g., teaching students to recognize the limitations of their own knowledge in science class, or to analyze sources for bias, deception, or manipulation in history class). These standards provide concise learning goals to help in planning integration. For instance, teachers could include

---

[4] For most core content areas, such as language arts and mathematics, higher levels of the education system (e.g., districts) will select curricula options for schools. Currently, though, many teachers report that they do not have ML guidance from their schools *or* districts, meaning that they often must make these decisions (Baker et al., forthcoming).

FIGURE 2.1

Truth Decay Media Literacy Standards

TRUTH DECAY

MEDIA LITERACY STANDARDS

Seeking a complete understanding of the facts

TRUTH DECAY **TREND** | **increasing disagreement about facts and analytical interpretations of facts and data**

1. Recognize limitations of one's own knowledge or understanding of the facts.
2. Use strategies to fill gaps in knowledge (e.g., connecting with experts on a topic; seeking information in a library; using search engines to find additional information).
3. Understand how modern information sources and tools can limit available facts and perspectives (e.g., search engine algorithms; specialized discussion groups; selection in social media connections).

Identifying trustworthy sources of information

TRUTH DECAY **TREND** | **declining trust in formerly respected sources of facts**

4. Identify the expertise (e.g., academic, office held, firsthand knowledge) and consider the motivations (e.g., political, financial) of the creator of an information product.
5. Evaluate whether information products meet established standards for process and presentation (e.g., scientific process, journalistic standards, peer review).
6. Analyze information for bias, deception, or manipulation.
7. Consider the social, political, and historical contexts of an information product and how those contexts influence meaning.

Evaluating the credibility of information and soundness of arguments

TRUTH DECAY **TREND** | **a blurring of the line between opinion and fact**

8. Understand the ways in which technology has the capability to undermine formerly trustworthy information products (e.g., audio and video "deep fakes").
9. Analyze whether evidence provided for an argument is adequate and can be independently confirmed; identify gaps in support or reasoning.
10. Compare multiple viewpoints on a topic and use evidence to determine how to manage discrepancies.
11. Recognize the ways that media and information products might trigger emotional responses that influence attitudes or elicit specific behaviors.

Responsible engagement to counter Truth Decay

TRUTH DECAY **TREND** | **the increasing relative volume and resulting influence of opinion and personal experience over fact**

12. Anticipate and monitor intended and unintended consequences of what is shared in digital spaces.
13. Recognize personal and cultural perspectives, particularly on controversial topics, and how those can influence interpretations of information.
14. Maintain openness to updating one's own views when presented with new facts or evidence.
15. Take action rooted in evidence (e.g., construct new knowledge, create and share media, engage in informed conversations and decisions about important issues).

an ML standard in each lesson plan *in addition* to their content-specific standards.

The ML standards can also be of use to those planning evaluations of ML educational interventions. When planning an evaluation, standards should influence the kinds of assessments—and what specific assessment items—to use when evaluating student learning outcomes. We recommend focusing on a particular shared group of competencies, such as those included in the Truth Decay ML standards, when designing research and measures for learning outcomes. We further discuss the importance of measures, and how standards relate to them, in Chapter Five.

More broadly than planning studies, working from a common set of standards could also help different ML evaluations "speak" to one another. We have previously identified wide-ranging ways that researchers conceptualize ML (i.e., through a lens of the economic motivations of media, the role of media in civic life and democracy, and tools for discerning information quality) (Huguet et al., 2019). The diversity of ways in which researchers define ML means that it is measured differently across studies, and aggregating findings is a challenge. If we can begin working from a common understanding of what we specifically are talking about when we research ML, evaluations could be of greater value in informing a larger body of work.

CHAPTER THREE

Exploring Conditions to Support Media Literacy Instruction

Phase	Planning for Implementation and Evaluation				Monitoring Implementation	Summative Evaluation
Step	Identifying ML learning expectations	Exploring conditions to support effective implementation	Selecting ML learning materials	Identifying measures of ML competencies	Monitoring interim progress	Measuring summative outcomes

As we will discuss in future chapters, clearly defined student learning expectations, thoughtfully selected instructional resources and materials, and appropriate measures of student mastery are all key components of high-quality ML education. However, implementation of ML is also influenced by a variety of additional conditions that can either support or hinder success. This chapter explores these conditions, highlighting those that may be particularly salient for successful implementation of ML instruction. The content of this chapter draws on the limited body of domestic and international ML education research. However, because research related to ML implementation is relatively narrow in scope, we supplement with a broader scope of literature. We draw on research regarding the implementation of instructional initiatives, such as SEL and digital and technology literacy, which can overlap in content, goals, and/or characteristics with ML. For instance, although SEL and ML address different skills, they share similarities in that they both tackle a complex set of competencies that can facilitate academic learning, even while sitting outside such core content areas as language arts or math. When relevant, we also intersperse content from a wider literature that focuses on implementation of educational initiatives broadly.

As discussed in more detail in the final section of this chapter, implementors can think about these conditions as guideposts when they consider how best to optimize the environment in which they will be implementing ML. Of course, implementors may not have direct influence over every condition described below; for example, teachers may not be able to control whether ML training is provided by their schools or districts. However, we believe this chapter can be a starting point for all implementors to be aware of the various factors that might affect ML implementation while also highlighting key conditions for success that may be within an implementor's purview. For evaluators—both internal, from schools and districts, and external—a clear understanding of these conditions can help inform the context of outcomes.

Conditions for Successful Media Literacy Implementation

We know that implementation moderates outcomes (Humphrey, Barlow, and Lendrum, 2018). In other words, the conditions under which an instructional initiative, such as ML education, is rolled out and put into practice on the ground will influence the outcomes of the initiative. We can think about factors that affect implementation as concentric circles, with layers of influence radiating from the focal topic—the instruction itself—outward (see Figure 3.1).[1] Nearest instruction, at the center, is the classroom, made up of students and teachers. The classroom is surrounded by the school, nested within the district and broader external environment (which encompass conditions in place at the community, state, and national levels). These layers interact, which can limit distinction between them: The dimensions that we discuss in this chapter often fit into more than one of these categories. This permeability is represented by the dashed lines in Figure 3.1 and

[1] This approach is a highly adapted and simplified version of Bronfenbrenner's ecological systems theory, which posits that individuals' development is influenced by a series of systems operating around them (Bronfenbrenner, 1981).

FIGURE 3.1
Select Implementation Conditions Affecting Media Literacy Instruction

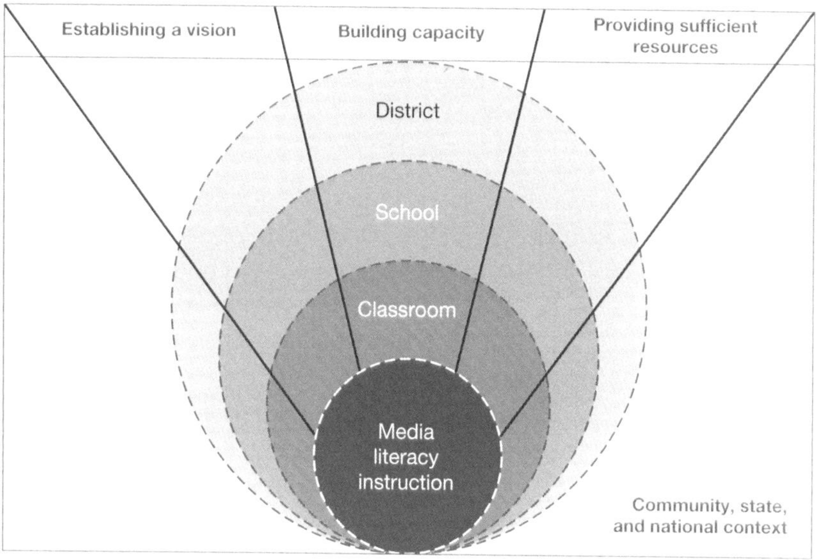

NOTE: This figure is not intended to be exhaustive

described in subsequent sections. With this layered structure in mind, we focus on three factors that—according to research—support implementation across levels: (1) establishing a clear vision, (2) building teacher capacity, and (3) providing sufficient resources for successful implementation. In each of these sections, we discuss the research related to these conditions at each layer. Thinking about instruction as situated at the center of this figure can help illuminate various considerations for implementation. Although we cover many implementation considerations in this chapter, we stress that our review is not exhaustive.

Establish a Clear and Shared Vision to Guide Successful Media Literacy Implementation

A clear and shared vision regarding ML educational goals—including why they are important and how they fit within the bigger picture of learning—

lays the foundation for successfully implementing ML programs. In the absence of such a vision, the wide array of potential goals for ML can lead to "incoherent expectations of outcomes" (Bulger and Davison, 2018). Furthermore, and as described later in this chapter, educators might interpret what ML means or what ML education should look like through the lens of their own background experiences and beliefs; therefore, a clearly defined vision of ML and its intended outcomes can support educators in making consistent and informed decisions about ML education in their schools (Mahoney and Khwaja, 2016). Establishing a coherent vision for instruction can include (1) explicitly defining what is entailed in an instructional initiative, (2) developing a common language around it, (3) agreeing on observable measures for success, and (4) outlining a strategic plan for implementation (Schwartz et al., 2020; National Commission on Social, Emotional, and Academic Development, 2019). This process takes time but can ultimately pave the way for stronger implementation (Schwartz et al., 2020). A clear vision can permeate every layer articulated in Figure 3.1; literature suggests that implementation can benefit from an instructional vision that is shared by stakeholders from all corners of the educational system, including school and district leaders, teachers, school staff, students and their families, and teacher educators (International Society for Technology in Education, undated; National Commission on Social, Emotional, and Academic Development, 2019).

A clear vision for ML at the classroom level is key, particularly because it can be difficult for teachers to find time for ML among the many competing priorities that they must balance on a daily basis. In a nationally representative survey, a majority of teachers reported that pressure to cover core required content, such as reading or mathematics, was an obstacle to promoting ML in their schools (Baker et al., forthcoming). These challenges may be especially salient when teachers perceive ML as extraneous to required content rather than integral to their overall learning goals for students (Schmeichel et al., 2018; Eickelmann, 2011).

To mitigate these challenges at the school level, school leaders can establish a schoolwide vision for ML education that frames ML as a helpful tool for supporting broader pedagogical outcomes rather than as an added or tangential burden on educators. Literature suggests that school leadership support may play a particularly crucial role in driving forward their school's vision for ML (Lorenz, Eickelmann, and Gerick, 2015; Eickelmann, 2011; Mahoney and Khwaja, 2016). Looking to related fields, we know that school leaders play a key role in establishing and sustaining a supportive climate for learning in their buildings (National Commission on Social, Emotional, and Academic Development, 2019; Allensworth and Hart, 2018). For example, research suggests that principals' technological leadership—which includes articulating a vision for technology in their schools—can in turn improve the technological literacy of their teachers and can encourage integration of technology into the classroom (Chang, 2012). A school leader with the influence to either empower or hinder ML efforts can be perceived as acting as a "green or red light for media literacy" (Deal, Flores-Koulish, and Sears, 2010, p. 128). Allensworth et al., describe principals as the "primary drivers of change in schools . . . [they] can serve as the bridge and the glue for the work that is happening across all classrooms" (Allensworth et al., 2018, pp. 26–27). By developing a vision that prioritizes ML as *part* of that work, school leaders set a tone that ML holds value for teaching and learning.

Of course, school leaders are not operating within a vacuum, and a supportive environment at the district level can also play a critical role in moving an instructional vision for ML forward. Although planning for instructional initiatives can sometimes bypass district involvement in the interest of time or ease, district leaders who are engaged from the outset can bolster both the momentum and the longevity of a specific initiative (O'Connor and Freeman, 2012). District leaders are also in a position in which they can explicitly show their support for an instructional vision through concrete policy and budget choices, strategic plans, and external communication (National Commission on Social, Emotional, and Academic Development, 2019).

Even beyond the classroom, school, and district, a clear vision can continue to support effective ML implementation. In the broader community, establishing a shared vision of ML with families may be of particular importance. Although educators can play a critical role in developing young people's ML skills, students are also absorbing messages and values about media at home and beyond. Challenges in ML education implementation may surface when these messages are in conflict (Deal, Flores-Koulish, and Sears, 2010), or when parents feel that schools are overstepping their role by teaching content that doesn't align with their own values (Hubbard, 2019). Teachers, school administrators, and district leaders can all help mitigate these challenges by establishing a clear vision, open lines of communication, aligned messaging, and active partnerships among families, schools, and communities to strengthen and reinforce learning across each of these settings (National Commission on Social, Emotional, and Academic Development, 2019; Hubbard, 2019; Jones and Kahn, 2017; Allensworth et al., 2018; Durand et al., 2016).

Build Teacher Capacity to Propel Successful Media Literacy Implementation

At the classroom level, the teacher has significant influence over student learning. Therefore, teacher capacity, which can encompass teachers' knowledge, skill, and comfort levels, is a critical piece of the implementation puzzle (Jones and Kahn, 2017). Providing teachers with ML training can build their capacity and ultimately play a key role in optimizing ML instruction for students (Webb and Martin, 2012).

Even when teachers have bought into the value of ML, they may lack the knowledge and skills to understand and apply its concepts for themselves (Deal, Flores-Koulish, and Sears, 2010; McGrew et al., 2018). This could lead to feelings of anxiety and insecurity for educators as they try to implement ML with students (Schmeichel et al., 2018; Garrett et al., 2020). Furthermore, broader implementation research suggests that the way a teacher interprets a directive and delivers instruction to students can be influenced by their own prior knowledge, past experiences, and beliefs (Coburn, Hill, and Spillane, 2016). This means that different teachers may interpret the same lesson plan in different ways, leading to inconsistent implementation. A focus on strengthening teachers' own ML skills and knowledge—and on surfacing or making explicit any preconceived biases or sociopolitical beliefs that teachers may hold about ML—can be viewed as a crucial step toward positioning teachers for consistent and effective ML instruction. This also comports with lessons from the field of SEL, where practitioners and researchers alike view the development of adult SEL skills as foundational to supporting student SEL (Schwartz et al., 2020; Jones and Kahn, 2017; National Commission on Social, Emotional, and Academic Development, 2019). Of course, building teacher capacity for implementing ML education is multilayered: In addition to developing their own ML skills, teachers must also have the necessary content knowledge and pedagogical skills required to make a set of complex and evolving concepts accessible to students (Deal, Flores-Koulish, and Sears, 2010). Furthermore, teachers must be familiar and comfortable with the specifics of the ML instructional materials they will be implementing with their students.

In spite of the importance of teacher capacity for implementing ML instruction, research suggests that teachers are currently not receiving adequate training in ML. In a nationally representative survey, a majority of teachers reported that a lack of ML training was an obstacle to promoting ML education (Baker et al., forthcoming). Similarly, most social studies teachers reported in a separate survey that they did not feel well prepared to support civic development in their students (Hamilton, Kaufman, and Hu 2020b).

Schools, districts, and states can all play a crucial role in building teachers' ML capacity by emphasizing the importance of—and providing opportunities for—teacher training and support around ML. Teacher capacity can be developed at multiple stages (e.g., training programs for new teachers, ongoing professional development [PD] for experienced educators) and through multiple mechanisms (e.g., teacher preparation programs, workshops, coaching, professional learning communities). Research shows that several key features comprise effective PD opportunities, including (1) incorporating active learning; (2) focusing on curriculum content and including guidance for differentiating content for diverse student needs; (3) supporting collaboration between teachers; (4) providing modeling, coaching, and feedback; (5) offering opportunities for reflection; and (6) sustaining educator development over time (Darling-Hammond, Hyler, and Gardner, 2017). Applying these same principles to teacher development in the field of ML will likely play a critical role in ensuring that ML efforts are implemented effectively.

In this section, we focus on building teacher capacity, in particular, because of teachers' direct role in implementing ML instruction in their classrooms. However, as with teachers, administrators' support for ML instruction may be influenced, or limited, by their personal beliefs and knowledge systems surrounding ML concepts (Mahoney and Khwaja, 2016). Therefore, ensuring that school and district leaders also have a solid foundation of ML knowledge and skills can support successful and sustainable ML implementation. Increasing school and district leaders' familiarity and engagement with ML concepts through capacity-building opportunities can support their efforts to, in turn, support the capacity of their students and teachers. Targeted PD can also lend itself to the clear and shared vision described in the previous section, by bringing educators schoolwide onto the same page, building common language and even buy-in to a particular initiative (Coburn, Hill, and Spillane, 2016).

Provide Sufficient Resources to Support Successful Media Literacy Implementation

Strategic partnerships and policies at the district, community, state, or national levels—including those related to funding streams and resource allocation, strategic and financial planning, or accountability and data systems—can play a critical role in bolstering school-level instructional initiatives (Eickelmann, 2011; International Society for Technology in Education, undated; National Commission on Social, Emotional, and Academic Development, 2019; Hamilton, Kaufman, and Hu, 2020a). On a theoretical level, the collaboration that can result from external and cross-sector partnerships can facilitate information exchange and knowledge-sharing across previously siloed efforts (Vinnakota, 2019; Bulger and Davison, 2018). On a practical level, strategic partnerships and policies can help unlock sufficient and equitable access to key resources in the classroom, school, district, and community. Such resources (e.g., technology infrastructure, funding, instructional materials) compose another critical element for the successful implementation of ML education.

The issue of technology access permeates almost every level of implementation. Given the nature of ML content, ML curricula is often (though not always) technology-dependent in that its implementation may benefit from access to devices and the internet; lack of, or uneven, access such resources can be a barrier to effectively implementing ML education (Lorenz, Eickelmann, and Gerick, 2015; Mahoney and Khwaja, 2016; Deal, Flores-Koulish, and Sears, 2010). Therefore, when using ML curricula that requires devices or internet, it is essential for classrooms to have access to enough technology, bandwidth, and technical support to accommodate all students (International Society for Technology in Education, undated), often funded at the district level. Even when schools have sufficient technology resources for their students, it is also critical that educators stay mindful of students' access to technology (and the quality of those access points) outside the school building. Although the digital divide in schools is shrinking, inequities in access to devices and internet at home persist and can affect the depth, frequency, and quality of students' interactions with technology (Blagg et al., 2020; Daugherty et al., 2014; Livingstone and Helsper, 2007). Of course, technology comes with costs, as can curriculum resources and teacher development. Therefore, the success of ML efforts can be derailed when there is insufficient or inconsistent funding to support them (Mahoney and Khwaja, 2016; Deal et al., 2010).

At the classroom level, access to high-quality ML instructional resources that meet the needs of teachers and students is also an important component of successful ML implementation. However, in a nationally representative survey, 57 percent of teachers reported that a lack of instructional resources was an obstacle to implementing ML (Baker et al., forthcoming). This suggests that teachers may need additional support from the school and district levels in selecting and/or procuring ML instructional materials. There are several factors that educators can consider in determining which resources may be the right fit in any given classroom. For example, the applicability of resources or curriculum used (Iachini et al., 2014) is a key consideration. To illustrate, consider a classroom of English-language learners. If the resource used is primarily written in English, a language that students in that classroom have little access to, their ability to learn and grow based on that resource may be limited. We discuss selection of ML instructional resources in more depth in Chapter Four of this report.

How This Chapter Can Inform the Implementation and Evaluation of Media Literacy Educational Efforts

These conditions for implementing ML, within and outside the school organization, are important to identify prior to implementation and to revisit throughout implementation. Though the conditions described in this chapter can act as guideposts for implementors, we recognize that stakeholders at different levels of implementation—from teachers to superintendents—will vary in terms of which factors they can (or should be expected to) control. Therefore, this chapter is intended as a starting point for implementors to identify the conditions that they may have influence over, and that can set the stage for high-quality implementation of ML. For example, school leaders might want to consider whether they have established and communicated a clear and shared vision of ML education within their building. District leaders may want to think about the technological resources currently available to teachers and students, and whether they are sufficiently and equitably distributed for ML education in the classroom. Teachers may also keep these conditions in mind when selecting instructional resources for their classrooms. For instance, if a school does not provide teacher training in ML, a teacher might seek an instructional resource that includes some form of capacity-building. Finally, knowledge of these dimensions may be helpful for implementors at every level who are advocating for additional or more-supported ML educational efforts in their schools, whether in the form of capacity-building and teacher training or in the form of developing a dialogue with parents about ML education.

These implementation conditions are informative for evaluators in two ways. First, identifying key implementation factors helps when designing an evaluation itself. Knowing what these factors are can allow evaluators to design data collection activities to monitor them, as detailed in Chapter Six. Second, these factors are valuable for evaluators because understanding the implementation of an educational intervention is key to contextualizing outcomes data and to identifying the successes, challenges, and resources required to successfully implement ML interventions. Knowing whether an intervention produced the desired outcomes means little if we do not understand the context for why. Whether a school leader has developed a clear vision around ML education, for example, or whether teachers receive adequate PD can add more-nuanced understanding about why a particular intervention did or did not produce the desired outcomes.

CHAPTER FOUR

Selecting Media Literacy Learning Materials

Phase	Planning for Implementation and Evaluation				Monitoring Implementation	Summative Evaluation
Step	Identifying ML learning expectations	Exploring conditions to support effective implemen-tation	Selecting ML learning materials	Identifying measures of ML comp-etencies	Monitoring interim progress	Measuring summative outcomes

This chapter is intended to aid in planning ML educational implementation by making the characteristics of available resources more visible; implementors, such as district decisionmakers, principals, instructional coaches, and teachers, can use the material here to consider the kinds of resources that might fit their particular needs at a point in time. When planning for the implementation or evaluation of any educational effort, it is critical to understand the types of instructional resources that will be used, if any. In a prior report, we highlighted the wide variety of ML resources that are publicly available (Huguet et al., 2019). This variety can present a challenge to implementors, as it is not always clear how these resources differ or where to begin the search. In a nationally representative survey of teachers, 56 percent of educators reported that a lack of clarity about resources was an obstacle to promoting ML in their practice (Baker et al., forthcoming).

This chapter outlines seven different dimensions on which ML resources can vary. Within the discussion of these dimensions, we highlight when research indicates that one type of resource is preferable to another. For instance, it might be necessary for a teacher to use a one-time ML lesson given their time constraints, but research suggests that longer-term interventions are more effective. We include a description of both one-time and longer-term resources, however, because we know that constraints on districts, schools, and teachers vary at different times; we recognize that there are instances when less-than-ideal resources must be used. This typology can help implementors think about their needs and constraints, and weigh those against what research highlights as preferable characteristics of instructional resources.

Evaluators can use this chapter in their planning for different reasons. The type of resources used in an intervention have real impacts on the ways that an evaluation is designed. For instance, if the resource at the heart of an intervention is primarily delivered by a teacher, it would make sense to collect interview or observational data from that teacher to better understand how the resource is implemented in actuality.[1] If a resource is instead delivered directly to students via an online learning portal, these data collection activities might be less relevant. We discuss at the close of this chapter ways that this typology can influence evaluation planning in the future.

Three clarifications are needed here. First, we refer to *resources* as opposed to *curricula* because we want to include other options, such as one-time instructional materials (e.g., videos or single lesson plans), online games for students to use directly, and materials to help teachers integrate ML into existing curricula. Second, it is important to note that this chapter should be used in the planning stages of implementation (to select resources) and evaluation (to design data collection activities), not as an evaluation of resources themselves. Finally, this chapter is not, in any way, intended to replace a thorough, formal curriculum selection process that district committees might undertake over an extended period. In most districts, these selection processes are in place for established content areas, and one day ML may join those ranks. However, at the time of this report, decisions about ML resources are often decentralized to the school and even classroom levels (Baker et al., forthcoming).

In the sections to follow, we present a tool—a typology of resources—that can orient implementors and evaluators to the kinds of resources avail-

[1] We discuss implementation monitoring in more depth in Chapter Six.

able. We describe each of the seven categories in our typology, then briefly explain how they can be useful to implementors and evaluators.

A Typology of Resources

Our typology, illustrated in in Figure 4.1, delineates seven dimensions of ML resources. The first six are primarily descriptive, but we emphasize that one side of a dimension may be clearly preferable. The seventh dimension of our typology—accessibility—is *not* simply descriptive. It is critical that all students are able to access an ML resource. Students' needs vary by classroom, so although we suggest some ways to consider whether a resource is accessible, users will also want to define for themselves how a resource can be most accessible to their students.

Category: Stand-Alone Versus Integrated

The first category addressed by this typology is stand-alone versus integrated. On one end of this spectrum, an instructional resource can be entirely stand-alone and not developed to integrate into an existing course. In this approach, ML is taught as its own content area. For instance, there may be separate time blocked off for an ML class one a day a week in which students receive focused lessons specifically about ML. Stand-alone ML

FIGURE 4.1
Typology of Media Literacy Resources

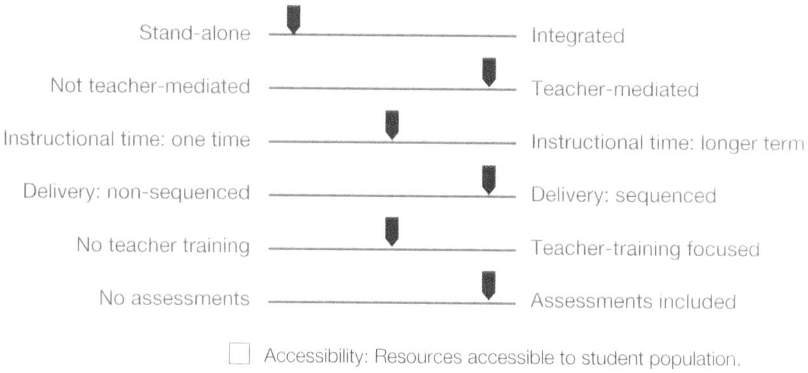

instructional resources do not need to be interwoven with existing non-ML curricula, such as science or reading, as stand-alone resources' primary goal is teaching ML itself and not relating to other content areas. Many of the ML instructional resources that are publicly available and easily accessible to educators are of this variety (Huguet et al., 2019). Stand-alone curricula may be easier to "assign" to specific teachers, allowing for more accountability in implementation. One challenge associated with this form of curricula is that teachers and schools need to find time in already overscheduled days to fit in an additional lesson or course; when ML is not a "tested" subject area on standardized state assessments, this may be difficult.

Some instructional resources fall somewhere between stand-alone and integrated on this spectrum, meaning that they can generally be taught without connection to another course but have been written with other content standards in mind. Linking ML to other content-area standards can help students "tap into the opportunity to develop robust foundations of learning supported by existing standards and subjects" (Cooper Moore and Redmond, 2014). Although these instructional resources can stand alone, it may be easier to find time integrating them in a demanding school schedule, as they can be used to teach standards for other content areas. There are several resources of this type available, such as Common Sense Education's Digital Citizenship Curriculum, which links each lesson to the Common Core State Standards (Common Sense Education, undated).

On the other end of this spectrum, ML instruction can be fully integrated into other content areas. People often think social studies and language arts curricula are most easily linked with ML competencies, but mathematics, science, and other subjects are also appropriate (Meehan et al., 2015; Media Literacy Week, 2020), as ML teaches students *how* to think, not *what* to think. ML includes thinking critically and synthesizing information, skills that can be embedded across all content areas. Experts advocate integrating ML into all curricular subjects as a way to demonstrate its applicability in all areas of life, so that it is not seen as isolated (Huguet et al., 2019). One example comes from Project Look Sharp at Ithaca College: they created a set of lesson plans organized by grade and subject area that specify how teachers can bring ML into their classes in sometimes unexpected ways (Project Look Sharp, undated). However, integrating ML into existing lessons requires a level of sophistication and knowledge on the part of teachers that may be challenging for educators with limited exposure to ML, or when new content-area curricula is introduced.

Category: Not Teacher-Mediated Versus Teacher-Mediated

ML instructional resources also vary by the degree of teacher involvement required. Some ML resources can be delivered to students directly via the internet or other media; if they were to be used in a classroom, a teacher could set students up on computers and allow them to guide themselves through modules or lessons. Students could also complete these lessons at home without the support of a teacher. For instance, Media Smarts has a series of online ML games that students can play on their own, including such titles as "Reality Check," which simulates social media and helps students learn to distinguish real news stories from false ones (Media Smarts, undated). Any instructional resource that is primarily delivered in this way would be categorized as *not teacher-mediated* in this dimension.

On the other end of the spectrum are instructional resources that are written exclusively for teachers to deliver to students, not necessarily blended with content, such as online modules, that students would complete independently. These resources may be considered more traditional in the sense that they can be delivered to a group by a lead instructor (such as a classroom teacher), and they can also be interactive. There are numerous examples of instructional resources in this format. For example, the NewseumEd provides several lesson plans related to media and news literacy that are complete with student worksheets, classroom resources (such as posters), and discussion questions (NewseumEd, undated). As we know student learning can be greatly shaped by teachers (Chetty, Friedman, and Rockoff, 2014), lesson delivery can depend on teacher training and skill (also noted in Chapter Three). Despite potential for variation, research suggests that teacher-mediated instruction is preferable to instruction that students engage in independently.

Category: Instructional Time, One Time Versus Longer Term

Although some instructional resources are designed as curricula that can be delivered over a semester or full school year, others are one-time lessons, videos, or activities. In this typology, instructional resources for use in a single sitting, class, or training are considered "one-time" resources. Research suggests that, while extended exposure to ML education is preferable (Jeong, Cho, and Hwang, 2012), even one-shot interventions—such as three-minute ML videos—may improve participants' ML competencies (Vraga et al., 2012; Vraga and Tully, 2015). As opposed to committing to a resource intended to be delivered over a longer period (e.g., a semester or a school year), some educators may find it more practical to deliver one-time ML instruction to their students. Although longer exposure to ML concepts could result in greater student mastery of ML concepts, this may be a practical necessity due to varying constraints on educators' time. In these cases, resources are available; for instance, the Critical Media Project from the University of Southern California's Annenberg School of Journalism provides a brief discussion of "DIY activities" that teachers could introduce in their classrooms—these can be focused on a single photograph, advertisement, or video clip, and can be used once or sprinkled throughout multiple lessons (Critical Media Project, undated).

On the other end of this spectrum are longer-term resources that are designed to be delivered over a period of class sessions, semesters, or full school years. For instance, Project Look Sharp provides several curricular units on various ML-related topics (e.g., media constructions of sustainability, a 19-lesson unit) that teachers can download from a website (Project Look Sharp, undated). Units that include multiple lessons could be delivered daily, weekly, or even monthly. In terms of efficacy, these are preferable to one-shot resources because there is evidence that longer-term interventions more effectively improve participant ML competencies than do short-term interventions (Jeong, Cho, and Hwang, 2012). However, educators might find it more difficult to set aside time for these extended interventions, particularly if the ML material is not integrated into existing courses.

Category: Non-Sequenced Versus Sequenced

Some instructional resources are offered as a sequence—a series of lessons or activities that should be delivered in order. Others have no explicit sequencing. No sequencing is common for one-time instructional resources, such as informational videos, that do not need to be tied to other lessons or videos. Resources that do not need to be delivered in a set order can provide flexibility for teachers to fit ML content into their activities when isolated time becomes available, or when they seem applicable to their focal content-area subject matter. TED-Ed, for instance, offers a selection of videos that could be used as one-time instructional resources and do not need to be linked to additional lessons (Tavlin, undated).

On the other end of the spectrum, some resources are intended to be delivered in sequence, without alteration. This is important when the content of one lesson builds on past lessons in a cumulative fashion. For instance, the Take Two Media Initiative, a New York-based nonprofit, helps teachers deliver filmmaking classes with an eye toward media literacy (Take Two Media Initiative, undated). Because their project-based approach has students create a video project, the lessons should be delivered in a sequence; for instance, revising a script comes before filming. One drawback of this format is that it requires educators to commit an amount of time for a series of lessons in advance, and some may find that challenging. On the positive side, students learning complex skills—such as those involved in ML—may benefit from content delivered in an intentional sequence so that it can build on itself or spiral back to reiterate important concepts.

Category: No Teacher Training Versus Teacher-Training Focused

ML instructional resources also vary in the degree to which they focus on teacher supports.[2] Some ML experts assert that training is critical for teachers to personalize ML education in their classrooms (Hobbs and Coiro, 2019). However, using a resource that does not include training does not mean that teachers will not receive ML training of any kind; PD can be pro-

[2] Resources that focus on teacher learning and student learning can be called *educative curricular materials* (Davis and Krajcik, 2005).

vided through other means. A benefit of accessing training with a particular resource is that it will likely be closely aligned with the content.

On one end of the spectrum, many instructional resources provide little or no teacher training at all. The majority of ML resources we have seen provide lessons for teachers to deliver to their students, or for students to explore on their own, but do not include any materials to build teacher capacity. Although teachers could benefit from PD in such content areas as ML, there is also some evidence that students still benefit from ML interventions even if their teachers have not received any training (Fingar and Jolls, 2014).

On the other end of this category, there are instructional resources that include some teacher training, though it is not the primary focus. We are not discussing pure PD resources in this section, as there are other considerations required to select those; rather, we are referring to instructional resources that also provide the teacher some degree of learning opportunity. There are some instructional resources, such as *Media Literacy: A System for Learning, Anytime, Anywhere* from the Center for Media Literacy, that offer teacher resources that help educators learn to integrate ML into their practice, in addition to ML lessons for use in the classroom (Center for Media Literacy, undated). Common Sense Education's Digital Citizenship Curriculum is another example of a resource that includes some teacher support, because they provide a video for teachers to watch in addition to the instructional materials (Common Sense Education, undated).

Category: Assessments Included Versus No Assessments

ML instructional resources also vary in whether they include a tool for educators to use in assessing student learning. Many resources do not provide any tools for assessment. For example, games and one-time ML videos often do not include an assessment of student learning. Instead, these resources can be used as tools that can be plugged into a teacher's broader vision for ML in a classroom.

Other ML resources include assessment tools that are aligned with instruction. These assessments may be multiple choice tests, rubrics to use when grading student work, or online quizzes. Measuring student learning is critical to knowing whether instructional resources and strategies are effective, as we discuss in upcoming chapters. By noting that these tools exist within a resource, our typology cannot gauge the quality of the assessment tools—only that they are available to assist educators in tracking student growth. Although teachers can create their own assessments, and ML quizzes can be found online disembodied from any curricular resources, those that come with an instructional resource should already be appropriately aligned with the content and save teachers the time of designing the assessment. For instance, Common Sense Education includes quizzes with their lessons so that teachers can track student learning. In Chapter Five, we discuss assessments in more depth, including the fact that the desired features of an assessment will depend on its intended use.

Accessibility

Our final category relates to the accessibility of ML resources, a dimension that will necessarily vary based on student population. Educators must reflect on the specific needs of the students they are working with when considering accessibility. Accessibility does not range from one end of a spectrum to another and, unlike the previous six categories that were simply descriptive (a resource leaning toward one end or another on the spectrum is not necessarily "good" or "bad"), accessibility is essential. There are four categories we draw attention to in relation to accessibility—language appropriateness, cultural relevance, developmental appropriateness, and technological accessibility—but, when selecting resources, there will be additional factors related to specific students' needs that are unique to each educator's or evaluator's situation.

The following considerations concerning accessibility of resources should be considered:

- *Is the resource available in the language(s) spoken by the students who will be using it?* Although some ML resources are published in multiple languages, there are also many that are provided in English-only formats. Language appropriateness is key so that students can access content. To the extent possible, users of the resources should verify the quality of the translation by seeking information on the expertise of the translators and the perceived quality of the translated materials among the target user groups.

- *Is the resource culturally relevant to the student population?* Research indicates that students who see themselves reflected in their educational curricula are more engaged with the content and often perform better on end-of-course assessments (Atwater, Russell, and Butler, 2013). Furthermore, the critical thinking that is central to ML education can provide an opportunity for critiquing power structures that often lead to the underrepresentation of minoritized groups in curricula (Aronson and Laughter, 2016). When selecting resources, one might ask: If the resource includes depictions of people, do those people have ethnic or cultural likenesses with the student populations? Will the topics discussed resonate with students?
- *Is the resource accessible to participating students' academic and developmental levels?* Students need resources that match their developmental stages; for example, a high school resource would likely not be accessible to students in elementary school. Furthermore, a group of students will likely include some individuals with special needs to consider, who may require some form of scaffolding or acceleration to engage with the resource; this also should be kept in mind when selecting resources.
- *Are the technological aspects of the resource accessible to the students who will be using it?* Many resources today can be accessed by students online, often independently. However, a portion of students in the United States do not have access to the kinds of technology at home (e.g., an internet connection, a computer or tablet) required to reach those resources (Blagg et al., 2020). If students are asked to use an online resource at home (e.g., watch a brief video or play an ML-related online game), it is important that all students have the tools to do so. This consideration emerged as particularly significant in the context of longer-term at-home learning experiences during COVID-19 school closures in 2020 and 2021.

How This Chapter Can Inform the Implementation and Evaluation of Media Literacy Educational Efforts

We designed this typology with implementors in mind. We hope district staff, principals, instructional coaches, and teachers will use the typology in their planning processes to consider the kinds of resources best suited for their particular needs. We invite implementors to use this typology to consider their own needs and constraints and weigh them against what research confirms are the best options for student learning. Because teachers often modify or create their own curricula, the seven categories in the typology can also support decisions about how to improve existing resources; for instance, a teacher might select a resource that students could use on their own but tweak it for greater teacher mediation. Modifications of this type are common in education and can be necessary to make a resource better suited for a particular classroom or activity. However, we must note that there is a risk to such modifications: If a program is evidence-based, any modification could reduce the likelihood that the positive effects demonstrated by research will be achieved.

For both internal and external evaluators, the type of resources used can have crucial implications for the design of an evaluation. For instance, in cases where ML is integrated into a broader content area (as opposed to a stand-alone ML lesson), it may be more challenging to observe implementation, or observations may need to occur over a longer period to locate instances of integration. In another example, if a resource is not teacher-mediated—for instance, if students are assigned to play an ML learning game online in the evenings—this will dictate again the degree of observations that can be completed, might introduce increased variation in how the resource is used at home, and might mean that the teacher's role in implementation is less focal than if they were directly delivering an ML lesson. Like these examples, each dimension of the typology discussed in this chapter holds implications for evaluation design. We hope that those developing evaluations of ML interventions will use these categories to consider what kind of data collection activities are best suited for their study.

CHAPTER FIVE

Identifying Measures of Media Literacy Competencies

Phase	Planning for Implementation and Evaluation				Monitoring Implementation	Summative Evaluation
Step	Identifying ML learning expectations	Exploring conditions to support effective implemen-tation	Selecting ML learning materials	Identifying measures of ML comp-etencies	Monitoring interim progress	Measuring summative outcomes

One of the most crucial dimensions of evaluating the effectiveness of ML education is high-quality measurement of ML competencies. The availability of appropriate ML measures is limited due to several factors, including a lack of agreement about how to define and operationalize ML, as well as shortcomings in widely used formats for assessing these competencies (Huguet et al., 2019). This has both empirical and practical implications, because it is difficult for implementors and evaluators to draw conclusions across the current evidence base (limited findings notwithstanding). Existing studies rely on different types of outcome measures, and many of them lack evidence of technical quality. In this chapter, we offer an overview of the state of the ML measurement field, provide examples of different types of existing measures, and discuss the significance of these considerations for implementors and evaluators.

Getting Measurement Right

Selecting appropriate measures and using them in the way that they were intended to be used are critical steps in any assessment context. Some measures described in research articles present reliability and validity evidence, but, in many cases, there is little or no evidence of the extent to which the assessment is well-suited to specific purposes, such as evaluating interventions or informing instruction. Other measures have been used in classrooms or schools to guide decisions about curriculum and instruction, but evidence of reliability and validity is often lacking. Users of assessments should clearly specify the purpose of the assessment, including the specific decisions its use will inform, before selecting or developing an assessment. [1]

The lack of widely available ML assessments with evidence of technical quality is due to several factors that make it difficult to measure ML competencies. First, as we discussed earlier in this report, ML involves a complex and varied set of competencies, and the field is constantly evolving alongside changes in the media and technology landscapes. The competencies relevant to ML do not always lend themselves well to traditional methods used in many standardized tests (such as multiple-choice format). And, as previously mentioned, there is a lack of common frameworks or standards that could help clarify the knowledge and skills that students with high levels of ML should be expected to demonstrate. In these ways, ML faces measurement challenges more similar to those in civic education or SEL (often referred to, fittingly, as "hard-to-measure competencies"; see Stecher and Hamilton, 2014), than in math and reading, where there is a longer history of large-scale assessment along with accepted sets of standards for which students should be tested. Clarifying *what* students should be tested on is one of the primary reasons we created our standards; we hope that having a clear, objective set of competencies will help support educators, policymakers, and researchers to develop higher-quality assessments that can be

[1] For additional guidance on how to interpret validity and reliability evidence to inform selection of educational assessments, see American Educational Research Association, American Psychological Association, and National Council on Measurement in Education, 2014; and Soland, Hamilton, and Stecher, 2013.

widely adopted across different contexts. In the next section, we will further discuss how students can be tested on these competencies.

Approaches to Measuring Media Literacy Competencies

As we discussed earlier in this report, and as illustrated in the standards we developed, ML competencies are numerous and varied. Consequently, a broad and varied set of assessments are needed to capture the full set of competencies. Decisions about measurement for a particular evaluation context should be informed not only by the purpose but by the specific learning goals and their amenability to measurement through different approaches. These approaches can be broadly categorized as follows:

1. self-reports or self-assessments (typically selected response), where respondents rate themselves on their own perceived competency levels
2. selected-response or short-answer assessments that require students to demonstrate competencies, including traditional multiple-choice exams
3. portfolios, which rely on collection of artifacts or work samples from students that are then evaluated, typically with a rubric
4. ratings of students' observable behaviors by an educator or other trained adult
5. direct assessments, where competencies are evaluated directly by having students/participants perform tasks and evaluating their performance in real time.

The boundaries among these categories are not always clear, and some assessments might incorporate multiple approaches. For example, a selected-response question that asks students how they would interpret results of an internet search would fit in both the second and fifth categories above. The specific category into which an assessment falls is less important than its suitability for a particular purpose and set of competencies. As we discuss in greater detail below, a given approach is likely to be suitable for some but not all of the competencies in the Truth Decay Media Literacy Standards (Huguet et al., 2021), and it can be especially helpful to consider the verbs with which each standard begins. For instance, standards that start with "understand" or "recognize" might need to be assessed through different kinds of items or tasks than ones that start with "evaluate" or "take action." In the rest of this section, we further explore two of the most common types of assessments—self-report assessments and direct assessments—and discuss their applicability to the ML competencies described in our standards.

Self-report measures ask what respondents would do in a hypothetical situation, or ask respondents to assess their own conception of how well they do something (hence, "self-report"). One good example of a self-report measure can be found in Literat, 2014, who created the New Media Literacies Questionnaire. The most relevant section of the questionnaire, titled "Judgment," includes the following questions:

- I can effectively determine whether or not the information I find online is correct and reliable.
- When I'm interested in a topic, I gather information from a bunch of different sources (like TV, radio, the internet, etc.) to try to get the full picture.
- When I search for something online and I get thousands of results, I can effectively decide which ones will be the most useful for me.
- I am able to enter the right words in a search engine to find what I am looking for.
- I can identify prejudice or bias in media (e.g., racism on certain websites, prejudice against women in song lyrics, etc.) (Literat, 2014, p. 27)

These questions can be answered with the following options: Strongly Disagree, Disagree, Neither Disagree or Agree, Agree, Strongly Agree. This is a classic example of a self-report measure, in which respondents judge their own ability based on the prompts and rate themselves according to a bipolar Likert scale. These items align—albeit imperfectly—with some of the Truth Decay Media Literacy Standards, such as "Analyze information for bias, deception, or manipulation" (Standard 6) and "Use strategies to fill gaps in knowledge . . . using search engines to find additional information" (Standard 2) (Huguet et al., 2021). These types of measures have several upsides: They are efficient, clearly understood, and easily scored and interpreted. However, there are also important downsides. Responses to these kinds of self-report items can be influenced by such biases as acquiescence bias (a tendency to agree with statements that are presented), halo effects (perceptions about one aspect influence perceptions of other aspects), social desirability (a tendency to respond in ways that reflect well on oneself), and recall difficulties (Schweig, Hamilton, and Baker, 2019). Taken together, these biases mean that respondents are not always very accurate in how they assess their own competency; therefore, results from self-report surveys should be interpreted with caution. Moreover, although these items arguably ask about competencies that are addressed in the Truth Decay Media Literacy Standards, they do not require students to demonstrate these capabilities. Therefore, the extent to which they are useful as measures might be limited, depending on the purpose and the desired inferences.

Direct (or "performance-based") assessments are designed to elicit behaviors from test-takers that closely align with real-world activities. These may be most effective in addressing Standards 4–9—for example, Standard 6, "Analyze information for bias, deception, or manipulation," would be best evaluated *directly* by a performance-based assessment (Huguet et al., 2021). Relatively few ML assessments directly evaluate student or participant competencies, though several efforts are underway to develop and validate such measures. We have identified three promising examples of performance-based assessments in ML for use as models going forward. The first, created and used by McGrew et al., 2018, is explained in Huguet et al., 2019 (p. 76):

> In one [example], students were given an article on the topic of the money habits of millennials; the author's byline states that he is an executive at a large national bank. The directions for students read, "Examine the document below and answer the question that follows," followed by, "This article argues that many millennials (people in their mid-20s to mid-30s) need help with financial planning. What is one reason you might not trust this article?" Student responses were scored using the team's developed rubric.

As this example shows, the respondents are being asked to react to a scenario and are evaluated based on how they judge or interpret the information. This relates directly to Truth Decay Media Literacy Standard 4 in Huguet et al., 2021, which emphasizes the importance of identifying expertise and considering motivations of the creator of an information product. The second example of a direct assessment can be found in Weber, 2012. In this study, students were given six "experiments," or tasks, that they had to respond to. Two examples of these tasks are explained in further detail here. In one task, students were split into two groups and read an article about a needle exchange program. The only difference between the two groups was the substance and source of a quote. In one group's article, the person quoted is described as "a researcher at the School of Public Health at the University of Maine," who discusses previous research on the topic. In the other group's article a "concerned citizen" provides a personal opinion on the topic. Students then went on to answer questions, such as:

- "How credible are the statements made by Rebecca Haag, the individual cited in the story?"
- "In the article, how strong is the evidence supporting the conclusion that the '1000 foot' rule will be ineffective in protecting children from drug areas?"
- "How reliable is the information in the article?" (Weber, 2012, p. 8)

In a second task, one group of students read a story on a current webpage, with working links to backup information presented; the second group of students read the exact same story, but on an outdated blog with no links. Students then responded to questions about the credibility of the story. These items relate directly to Truth Decay Media Literacy Standard 9 in Huguet et al., 2021, which emphasizes considering the source and credibility of evidence for an argument.

The third and final example comes from McGrew et al., 2019, in which students were shown different media items and then asked to evaluate them. The items on this assessment elicit student responses that demonstrate competencies represented in several of the Truth Decay Media Literacy Standards, including those related to evaluating the credibility of information and responsible engagement. In one case, McGrew et al. scored students on a three-point rubric based on their (open-ended) evaluation of the legitimacy of a photo posted on Twitter, with students achieving a 2 score ("Emerging") if they raise questions about the legitimacy of it but do not dive deeper, and a 3 ("Mastery") if they question the source of the post and/or the source of the photograph. In another example, they score students based on their evaluation of the legitimacy and credibility of a webpage on a specific website (such as "unionfacts.com" or "acsh.org"). Taken together, these items relate directly to Standards 4, 6, 7, and 9 in Huguet et al., 2021, which all emphasize the importance of identifying credible and trustworthy sources of information. Furthermore, the authors found these and related assessments to function well in an evaluation measuring the effects of a curriculum—a promising example of these types of assessments being used in real classrooms.

All three of these direct, performance-based measures could be helpful for documenting the effectiveness of an intervention or program that is designed to influence students' behaviors in ways that would be difficult to measure through self-reports or other commonly used assessment approaches. This type of measurement tool is certainly less efficient from both a respondent and scoring standpoint, but is a promising mechanism to more adequately capture actual competencies.

As we show in Table 5.1, each of these assessment types has its own advantages and limitations. Users will need to consider their specific context and constraints in addition to the purposes for which they intend to use the data. A brief, multiple-choice measure might be adequate for gathering data on students' ML knowledge at a fairly high level, whereas a more expensive or time-consuming format might be needed to measure more complex skills. In addition, existing assessments might need to be adapted based on age group, level of access to technology, and other contexts to meet users' needs, but such adaptations could threaten the technical quality of the assessment and should be done cautiously.

TABLE 5.1

Assessment Types, Strengths, and Weaknesses

Assessment Type	Description	Strengths	Limitations
Self-reports or self-assessments	Respondents rate themselves on their own perceived competency levels (typically selected response)	Efficient and practical (i.e., relatively straightforward to implement and requires little or no specialized equipment or training)	Potentially inaccurate and susceptible to bias
Selected-response or short-answer assessments	Require respondents to demonstrate competencies, including traditional multiple-choice exams	Efficient and practical (i.e., relatively straightforward to implement and requires little or no specialized equipment or training)	Not suitable for capturing evidence of students' actual behaviors; provides limited evidence regarding complex skills and deep knowledge
Portfolios	Rely on collection of artifacts or work samples from students that are then evaluated, typically with a rubric	Allows for direct review of student work; can capture evidence of a variety of ML competencies	Time- and labor-intensive to score; scores influenced by the expertise and training of those who provide ratings
Observer rating	Ratings of observable behaviors by an educator or other trained adult	Allows for direct review of student behavior	Time- and labor-intensive to carry out ratings; requires expertise of observer
Direct assessments (also referred to as "performance assessments")	Competencies are evaluated directly by having students or participants perform tasks and evaluating their performance in real time	Allows for direct review of student competency	Typically require extensive administration time and/or equipment and materials; scoring might require human raters, which introduces costs and potential bias and subjectivity

How This Chapter Can Inform the Implementation and Evaluation of Media Literacy Educational Efforts

Regardless of the subject matter, educators need information about how well students are mastering the content so that they can adjust their instruction to meet individual- and classroom-level needs. Implementors, such as teachers, might use these data to identify students who could benefit from supplemental instruction or who are ready for more-advanced content. These data can also help district decisionmakers, principals, instructional coaches, and teachers discern the effectiveness of an instructional approach or intervention and to identify groups of students who might benefit from a new or different approach.

Of course, teachers, principals, and instructional coaches are constantly gathering data on student learning through self-developed assessments and informal monitoring of students. Students' questions, participation in discussions, and level of engagement all generate data to inform instruction. At the same time, data gathered through systematic, externally developed assessments, such as the example assessments discussed above, can provide a valuable source of information for teachers, and such assessments are commonly used for this purpose in academic subjects, including mathematics and language arts. High-quality, externally developed measures of students' ML competencies can be particularly helpful if district decisionmakers, principals, instructional coaches, or teachers are interested in examining performance and trends across different classrooms or schools, and such measures can also facilitate efforts to monitor changes in performance over time.

To be useful for the purposes of informing instruction, assessments should have evidence of validity and utility for that purpose. Desirable features include scoring methods that teachers can implement relatively easily (e.g., automated scoring that produces immediate results, or a scoring rubric that allows teachers to assign scores to their own students), along with guidance that links scores or performance profiles to concrete next steps for instruction. If the purpose is to assess learning that is tied to a specific curriculum or program, using an assessment that is packaged with that curriculum or program can be helpful and might be the most feasible types of assessments to adopt. At the same time, it can be beneficial to supplement with other measures that are not tied to that curriculum to understand the extent to which learning generalizes or to predict how students will perform in other contexts.

For evaluation purposes at a larger scale, such as at the school or district level, assessment users should gather evidence that functions similarly across different contexts and for all student groups who will be included in the assessments. Issues of fairness are particularly salient, because an assessment that lacks validity for some groups will lead to inaccurate inferences about group performance. It is also important that assessments for monitoring produce scores and reports that are easy to interpret, and that the constructs measured by the assessment align with school- or system-level goals or standards so that the data from the assessments are useful for informing decisionmaking (see Chapter Two for the Truth Decay ML standards). Finally, inferences about how student performance changes over time, such as before and after the implementation of an ML curriculum module, should be based on assessments for which there is validity evidence regarding the use of change scores.

Finally, to advance the ML educational evidence base, it will be crucial that future studies clearly define the ML constructs of interest within the specific intervention being studied and that the appropriate assessments are administered to measure these constructs. When evaluating evidence of reliability and validity for intended uses, researchers should be especially attuned to evidence that the assessment measures the competencies that the intervention aims to improve, and that this evidence was gathered in a context that is similar to the one that the researcher will be studying. In particular, there is a need for evidence gathered from a similar student population, demonstrating that the assessment functions equivalently across different student groups (e.g., racial/ethnic, gender, and spoken language, where relevant). The accessibility considerations discussed in Chapter Four are applicable to assessments and instructional resources.

CHAPTER SIX

Monitoring Interim Progress

Phase	Planning for Implementation and Evaluation				Monitoring Implementation	Summative Evaluation
Step	Identifying ML learning expectations	Exploring conditions to support effective implementation	Selecting ML learning materials	Identifying measures of ML competencies	Monitoring interim progress	Measuring summative outcomes

Monitoring is important for those implementing ML education. It can help them understand the degree to which their efforts are being undertaken as intended, identify factors that might be helping or hindering their work, and support improvement over time. Monitoring data can help educators course-correct or adjust instruction and provide lessons for future implementation. Monitoring implementation is key to continuous improvement efforts undertaken at every level of the educational system, including the classroom, school, district, and beyond.[1]

Studying implementation is also an important dimension of a thorough evaluation. Evaluators can look to monitoring data for indicators about how implementation is progressing, for lessons learned about conditions and contexts that best support an intervention, and for insights into outcomes

[1] *Continuous improvement* is a process of monitoring and iterating on implementation of new strategies, used across sectors. In education, "Continuous improvement can refer to a school, district, or other organization's ongoing commitment to quality improvement efforts that are evidence-based, integrated into the daily work of individuals, contextualized within a system, and iterative" (Best and Dunlap, 2014).

data. Monitoring data might reveal, for instance, that teachers at one school did not have the time to implement an intervention as designed; if outcomes show that students at that school did not perform as well as others, knowing that instructional time was a constraint can provide important contextual information. However, it is important to note that monitoring data are also useful independent of outcomes data, because such information can shed light on challenges and successes of an intervention from the perspective of those most closely involved (e.g., teachers).

There are two ways we discuss monitoring the progress of ML educational efforts in this chapter. The first is through FA of student learning. The second is through the collection of broader qualitative data, such as interviews and observations. We explain these approaches in the sections that follow, then briefly delve into how implementors, in particular, can leverage monitoring data for continuous improvement. Finally, we again visit how information in this chapter can be of value to both implementors and evaluators.

Formative Assessment

Although summative assessments measure final student learning at the end of a course, FAs track student progress. Educators often consider FAs to be assessments *for* learning, versus assessments *of* learning. In other words, FA outcomes are used to inform and adjust and improve instruction and learning rather than providing a final account of student learning.[2] Assessments are formative "to the extent that evidence about student achievement is elicited, interpreted, and used by teachers, learners, or their peers, to make decisions about the next steps in instruction that are likely to be better, or better founded, than the decisions they would have taken in the absence of the evidence that was elicited" (Black and Wiliam, 2009, p. 9). For instance, FA might include providing feedback on work so that students can adjust, making changes to lesson plans, or promoting classroom dialogue for peer learning and engagement. The assessment itself can take many forms—from all of the more-formal assessment types discussed in the previous chapter to

---

2 See Chapter Seven for information about summative assessment of student learning.

informal "thumbs-up" check-ins during instruction—because it is not the format of the assessment that makes it formative, it is how the data are used.

Educators and evaluators can employ FAs throughout the implementation of an intervention to gain understanding of progress toward final learning outcomes. The FA measures used (the content and design of weekly quizzes, for instance) will be most useful if they closely align with measures eventually used to assess final outcomes (e.g., the questions on an end-of-term test) (Bennett, 2011).

In the classroom, teachers can use FAs to immediately change interactions with students or to alter longer-term planning. This distinction is sometimes referred to as synchronous versus asynchronous FA (Black and Wiliam, 2009). Synchronous FAs can help educators make quick adjustments to instruction; for example, if a teacher selects students at random to answer questions during class, and some students offer responses that clearly indicate misunderstandings, the teacher might immediately slow or reframe instruction, set up group work where students can learn from one another, or provide one-on-one attention to students who misunderstood the concept. Teachers use this kind of quick FA on a moment-to-moment basis in their instruction (Antoniou and James, 2014).[3] Asynchronous FA, in contrast, influences longer-term planning. For instance, a teacher might create weekly quizzes in advance, analyze students' scores on them to better understand their comprehension, and update the next week's instruction based on data from those quizzes. Evaluators' FAs would typically fall under the category of asynchronous, or planned in advance.

Educators and evaluators can design FAs to monitor specific content knowledge as well as learning skills. "The aims of any instruction are usually a combination of aims specific to the subject and aims directed to improving learning skills. For many teachers, the former are explicit and the latter only implicit" (Black and Wiliam, 2009, p. 18). In the case of ML, learning skills often are explicit by nature; ML competencies are not linked to traditional core content areas (e.g., knowing specific terminology or mathemati-

[3] However, these kinds of adjustments can lead to variation in implementation; unlike implementors, evaluators typically seek consistency in implementation so that outcomes reflect the results of the curriculum or program as intended rather than reflecting teacher-by-teacher differences.

cal formulas), but instead relate to the ways that students think about the information that they receive and share in the world. In other words, ML education does not teach what to think, but how to think. For example, one of the Truth Decay ML standards is "Maintain openness to updating one's own views when presented with new facts or evidence" (Huguet et al., 2021, p. 4). Measuring learning skills, such as the one described in this standard—process-related skills—can present a challenge because they are often complex. For more about measuring such skills, see Chapter Five.

Monitoring Implementation Using Qualitative Data

Although conducting FAs of student learning is valuable, additional qualitative data about the implementation of a learning initiative provide feedback from a different perspective. These data are not focused on student learning but on the process of enacting a particular intervention. There are numerous ways to collect implementation data; we discuss surveys, interviews, focus groups, observations of instruction and/or PD, and document collection, as well as some benefits and drawbacks of each of these approaches (see Table 6.1). Using multiple approaches to data collection is necessary to confirm findings across multiple stakeholders or formats—often called *triangulation* (Patton, 1999)—and develop a more complete picture of implementation. We provide highly simplified explanations in this chapter and suggest further reading before undertaking evaluations.

Survey data can provide aggregate information about how individuals involved with implementation interpret the progress of an initiative. Surveys can ask questions about topics in each of the concentric circles identified in Figure 3.1. For instance, an evaluator could field a survey to implementing teachers to ask about their perspectives of the classroom (e.g., the degree to which students engage with a curriculum, which dimensions of the curriculum are easiest or most difficult to implement), their school (e.g., their perspectives about school-provided PD, what kinds of messages their school leadership provides about an initiative), or outside support (e.g., what reactions have they received from parents). Surveys have the benefit of reaching a broad audience with relative ease; particularly given modern online survey platforms, it can be inexpensive to gather data from a large

TABLE 6.1

Qualitative Data Collection Activities for Monitoring Implementation

	Surveys	Interviews	Focus Groups	Observations	Document Collection
Benefits	• Inexpensive • Anonymous • Wide-reaching	• Open-ended questions • Opportunities to probe	• Open-ended questions • Opportunities to probe	• Not rooted in participant perspectives	• Efficient • Easy to compare with other data sources
Drawbacks	• Predetermined • Limited answers	• Limited anonymity • Time consuming	• Limited anonymity and confidentiality • Time consuming	• Time consuming	• Limited usability
Tools required	• Survey items • Survey platform	• Interview protocol	• Focus group protocol	• Observation protocol (e.g., rubric or checklist)	• None
Can answer questions, such as...	• What percentage of teachers report that their ML training was effective?	• To what degree do teachers buy into an ML education initiative, and why? • What challenges do teachers face when implementing an ML resource?		• Is an ML resource being delivered as written? • Do students appear engaged?	• How many teachers attended a particular PD? • What is the focus of ML lesson plans?

group using this method (Ponto, 2015). Survey data can also be anonymous, which can be of particular importance if an evaluation is conducted by a participant's supervisor in their school, district, or other entity. Anonymity is important for gathering candid insights. Furthermore, the consistent response options in surveys lend themselves to analyzing disaggregated data and longitudinal data that may be harder to do with other kinds of implementation data. Drawbacks of using surveys include that they typically offer predetermined answer options rather than allowing respondents to provide original insights, and they do not provide immediate opportunities for probing deeper into responses.

Interviews and focus groups provide opportunities for in-depth questioning about participant experiences. Interviews include one respondent answering questions, similar to the way that surveys collect feedback from individuals. In contrast, focus groups include multiple participants; this can have both benefits and drawbacks. In a focus group, participant responses may play off of one another in ways that expose new ideas (Harrell and Bradley, 2009). However, it is not possible to guarantee confidentiality of responses (though it can be encouraged) and some respondents may not be as forthcoming in a group setting (though some studies suggest that as much or more sensitive information comes from focus groups as interviews; see Guest et al., 2017). There are benefits to interviews and focus groups that surveys do not offer. Of note, questions posed in interview and focus group protocols are preferably open-ended, meaning that respondents can answer in a plethora of ways rather than selecting from evaluator-created options; this means that responses may be more nuanced, and unexpected findings can emerge from the data (Adams, 2015). Interviewers can probe responses in the moment when doing interviews, soliciting greater detail about participants' perspectives. There are also opportunities for participants to provide examples or anecdotes that can add depth to evaluators' understanding of how implementation is playing out on the ground. However, interviews and focus groups are difficult to conduct anonymously; if someone in a supervisory role manages an evaluation, participants may not be comfortable providing forthright responses to all questions. In addition, conducting interviews and focus groups and analyzing their resulting data are time-consuming and can lead to higher costs than surveys.

Observations are different from surveys, interviews, and focus groups in that they do not seek perspectives from participants but instead document the actual unfolding of events in situ. For instance, when conducting an evaluation of an ML intervention, observing the ML instruction in classrooms should be a focal activity. We recommend that an observer use a protocol designed to highlight dimensions of interest; the observation protocol could look like a rubric, in which the observer rates predetermined categories of the lesson that relate to the goals of the intervention (e.g., the degree to which a teacher followed the lesson plan as designed, or the proportion of time that students spent engaging in group work, teacher direct instruction, or individual work). Observation protocols exist for many subject areas,[4] although, at this time, we are not aware of existing observation protocols specific to ML instruction. ML observation rubrics, validated across multiple types of classrooms, would be an important addition to the field and improve implementation monitoring. Many evaluations of school- or district-level initiatives will include observations of teacher training, as well as instruction. Although collecting participant perspectives is important, observations are valuable because they allow the evaluation team to see what is happening on the ground for themselves, free of participants' lenses. Observations are not objective—as the observers themselves bring a particular frame of reference to data collection—but they are a more direct way of understanding how an effort is progressing (Merriam and Tisdall, 2015). However, they are subject to some of the same shortcomings that interviews and focus groups are; observations are time consuming, and participants may change their behavior because they know they are being observed. Furthermore, consistent training can help observers align their ratings, but there is no way to ensure full alignment across individuals.

Finally, document collection can augment the other data collection activities mentioned earlier (see Bowen, 2009, for further details). This is self-descriptive; before, during, or after other data collection activities, evaluators request documentation related to the ML intervention. These documents can be wide-ranging (Bretschneider et al., 2017); in the case of evaluating a school-level ML intervention, they might include lesson plans, records

---

[4] See, for example, the Best Practices in Social Studies Rubric from the Iowa Department of Education (Iowa CORE, 2018).

of PD attendance, handouts or presentation slides used during PD, and even examples of student work. Document collection can be a time-effective way to gather additional data about implementation. Documents can be used to triangulate information gathered via interviews and observations. It can also be useful to collect documents prior to other data collection activities, such as interviews, to reference them during the interviews themselves. For instance, if an evaluator were to collect a series of handouts from attending a PD session, the evaluator could bring these handouts to an interview and ask the participant to explain them or request other details about how they were used. That said, documents can be limited in their usability; before collecting documents, the purpose of their collection should be identified.

There are several considerations to keep in mind for each of these approaches to monitoring implementation. Each form of data collection requires the thoughtful development of tools, such as interview protocols, and other processes (e.g., participant selection). Another consideration is that each of these activities requires intentional systems for collecting and organizing data, an important and often overlooked step that is necessary for systematic data analysis. For example, evaluators must consider whether they will take notes during interviews, and/or record and transcribe interviews, and where that data can be stored securely.

Notably, in all cases, participants must be fully aware of their participation and any related risks, and explicitly consent. Depending on the particular context of the evaluation, these activities may also need to be cleared through a school district's internal review board—the body formally designated to protect human subjects involved in research activities.

Using Monitoring Data for Continuous Improvement

Data collection activities should not be the final step—data are useful only so far as they influence changes or inform broader findings. For teachers, using data often translates into changing instruction in some way. For evaluators who are at the school or district levels, data can also inform changes, such as working to improve organizational factors that influence implementation or updating preferences when selecting curricula.

There is a robust body of research exploring ways that teachers collect and use data to inform continuous improvement. Ideally, they would undertake a cyclical process in which teachers interpret data into information and actionable knowledge, implement change based on that knowledge (e.g., address individual student needs, assess progress toward goals), and collect data again to determine how their changes affected the outcomes of interest (Hamilton et al., 2009; Marsh, Pane, and Hamilton, 2006). High-level findings from research on teachers' data use suggest that we cannot assume that teachers have the capacity to make use of the data they collect naturally, rather, they need PD and supports to do so (Datnow and Hubbard, 2016; Jimerson and Wayman, 2015). In addition to trainings, principal and/or coaching support can bolster data-use efforts (Datnow, Kennedy-Lewis, and Park, 2013; Huguet et al., 2014; Marsh and Farrell, 2015). Working in peer groups or professional learning communities may also benefit teachers in using collected data to alter instructional practice (Van Gasse et al., 2017). Like other educational practices, the ways that teachers use data are influenced by their own backgrounds, experiences, and beliefs (Farrell and Marsh, 2016; Jimerson, 2014).

How school and district leaders respond to implementation data depends on the specifics of the evaluation, the context in which they operate, and—like teachers—their individual backgrounds and beliefs. Some experts assert that having a clear vision around evidence use at the school or district level is an important condition for making informed decisions (Wayman, Jimerson, and Cho, 2012). Studies also indicate that principals are more likely to use evidence in their decisionmaking when it is generated from within their own schools—such as when they are monitoring implementation themselves—but feedback from an external evaluation can be as useful (Demski and Racherbäumer, 2015). School and district leaders can engage in inquiry cycles, as teachers do, though they may be using different information and making different kinds of decisions (Hough, Kalogrides, and Loeb, 2017).

How This Chapter Can Inform the Implementation and Evaluation of Media Literacy Educational Efforts

Monitoring is critical to both the implementation and evaluation of ML interventions. Most educators already integrate FA into their practice, whether that is via informal checks for understanding or more-formal pen-and-paper assessments (e.g., weekly quizzes) throughout a unit. Although less often considered in classroom-level data use, other forms of implementation monitoring are also applicable to teachers; teachers can learn from interviewing or surveying students, even informally, about their experience using an ML resource. These data can be made useful through continuous improvement and data use efforts. For implementors who are supporting teachers in their ML instruction, such as district and school leaders and instructional coaches, the kinds of information to emerge—not only from student FAs, but from interviews, observations, and document collection—can inform policies and guide change at multiple levels.

Evaluators—whether they are internal to the school or district or external partners—will be familiar with the implementation monitoring described in this chapter. Evaluations of school- and district-level initiatives typically include some or all of the qualitative measures outlined earlier. These data are valuable in and of themselves; they can independently inform changes to implementation and instruction, shed light on challenges and successes of an intervention from multiple perspectives, and support a richer understanding of an intervention. For evaluators, monitoring data are also valuable when paired with outcomes data; the implementation data described in this chapter can provide context for why some classrooms, schools, or districts result in better or worse student learning outcomes despite using the same instructional resources. Pairing these kinds of data is important for identifying what factors might best support similar interventions. In the following chapter, we discuss summative evaluation of student learning.

CHAPTER SEVEN

Evaluating the Effects of Media Literacy Instruction

Phase	Planning for Implementation and Evaluation				Monitoring Implementation	Summative Evaluation
Step	Identifying ML learning expectations	Exploring conditions to support effective implementation	Selecting ML learning materials	Identifying measures of ML competencies	Monitoring interim progress	Measuring summative outcomes

The final step in the implementation and evaluation framework is to use data from summative assessments to evaluate whether, or by how much, the overall program of ML instruction resulted in students meeting the defined learning expectations. This contrasts with using FAs to track interim progress and the effects of the instructional program before it has been completed. Such a summative or outcomes evaluation might be performed by a variety of actors. For example, school or district staff may conduct an evaluation for internal purposes to confirm whether the objectives of implementation were met; or an external evaluator may seek to generate more-general evidence that will be useful to a broad audience of educators and policymakers interested in effective ML instruction. In this chapter, we describe methods of analyzing test scores that do not require specialized expertise, with discussion of some more-sophisticated methods in the appendix. A key objective of summative evaluation is to discern whether the ML program *caused* the measured results. This chapter discusses two key evaluation features that affect this ability to make causal attribution: the selection of a summative assessment and the evaluation design. As discussed in

Chapter Six, information collected as part of implementation monitoring can be useful in helping to interpret the program effects estimated through outcomes evaluation.

Summative Assessment

Evaluating the effects of an instructional program on student competencies requires a summative assessment administered at the end of the program. Here, we briefly recap some salient points about assessment that are discussed in greater detail in Chapter Five. For a summative assessment to be useful for evaluation, it should seek to measure student attainment of the goals or standards defined for the instructional program. Although an assessment packaged with the curriculum can meet this criterion, it can be especially helpful to use one designed for more-general purposes, if available, to help understand the extent to which learning generalizes. Moreover, as will be discussed later in this chapter, stronger evaluation designs rely on comparing assessment results of students who were exposed to the curriculum with results from students who were not. An assessment packaged with the adopted ML program could frame questions in ways that echo instructional materials, inadvertently advantaging students who were exposed to those materials, and thus biasing estimates of the program's effects on learning. Chapter Five also discusses other features of assessments that are desirable for summative evaluation. Making a good choice of summative assessment is important for each of the evaluation design options discussed next.

Evaluation Design

Although a primary goal of a summative evaluation is to assess whether the desired learning objectives have been met, other questions about the effectiveness of the instructional program are also relevant to a varying extent depending on whether the evaluation is for internal purposes of a school or district, or for a broader audience. For example, the value of the instructional program cannot be fully determined by simply showing that students know the material at the end of the program. Perhaps they already knew the material before the program started, or would have learned the material even if the instructional program had not been adopted. Thus, evaluations often use a pretest to gauge performance before exposure to the program, and may also gather pre- and posttest data from a comparison group of students who were not exposed to the program.

Here, we lay out four research designs that are progressively stronger in terms of the evidence they can produce (see Table 7.1). Although these are not the only available research designs, they are the most common and straightforward to implement. We describe a bare-bones version of each design, and an appendix describes some methodological or analytic enhancements, including testing whether a program effect estimate is statistically significant. We present several research designs because, although a randomized controlled trial is the strongest, its requirements may make the design undesirable or infeasible in some circumstances. Other designs may be more appropriate, and we simply encourage choosing the strongest from among those appropriate for the situation at hand. For the two stronger research designs, we discuss the ability for the evaluation to meet What Works Clearinghouse standards (Institute of Education Sciences, 2020) and the evidence tiers defined in the Every Student Succeeds Act (ESSA) (U.S. Department of Education, 2016). If the ML program is fully developed and ready for broader use, meeting these levels of evidence could potentially unlock avenues to obtain funding for scale-up and be influential toward other districts' decisions whether implement the program.

TABLE 7.1
Research Design Types and Features

Rigor	Research Design Type	Features of Design
Less	Posttest only	Can demonstrate skill attainment at endpoint but change in skills or that ML curriculum taught those skills
	Pretest-posttest	Can demonstrate skill growth and attainment, but cannot attribute these to the ML curriculum
	Comparison group	Can demonstrate skill growth and attainment, and weakly attribute these to the ML curriculum, with risk of bias
More	Randomized controlled trial	Can demonstrate skill growth and attainment, and strongly attribute these to trial the ML curriculum

Posttest-Only Design

In a posttest-only design, the summative assessment is administered to students after they complete the ML instructional program. This design enables the evaluator to confirm whether students have accomplished the learning objectives that were established during planning the ML program implementation. However, it cannot demonstrate that the ML instructional program was what caused the students to reach the learning expectations or the amount of learning for which the program was responsible. First, without a pretest, it is not directly evident whether students already knew the material before the program started. Second, even if they did not know the material before the program started, without a comparison group, it cannot be ruled out that some other process caused the students to learn the material during the time the program was underway. This could occur, for example, if ML concepts were taught in other courses or if students naturally developed the concepts through maturation or their everyday experiences.

Although these limitations make this design undesirable for generating useful evidence for a broad audience, school or district administrators may find it sufficient for internal purposes if they can triangulate the evaluation results with other data. For example, if, prior to implementing the ML instructional program, students consistently demonstrated poor ML skills, simply determining that those skills are evident after implementing the program may be deemed sufficient for crediting the program for that change. This is particularly compelling if no other curriculum changes occurred that might be responsible. Moreover, data gathered during implementation monitoring may bolster confidence that the attainment of the learning objectives were induced by the program. For example, teachers may report that students demonstrated progress on FAs, assignments, or class performance that coincided with curriculum coverage of the relevant material.

Pretest-Posttest Design

Adding a pretest can strengthen the evaluation by demonstrating that student skills increased over the course of the instructional program. In this design, it is desirable for the pretest and posttest to produce scores on the same scale—that is, both tests would produce the same numeric score for a given level of student skills—so that the difference in scores represents learning growth that occurred between the two assessments. In the relatively nascent landscape of ML assessment, this is most likely accomplished by administering the same assessment or alternate forms of the same assessment at both timepoints.[1] A caution about using the identical assessment twice is to ensure that sufficient time has elapsed so that students are unlikely to improve simply because they remember the items from the prior administration.

With scores on the same scale, simply subtracting the pretest from the posttest for each yields a growth score for each individual, which can then be averaged across students to obtain a measure of average growth for the student population. A positive result provides evidence that, on average, students learned the material during the time that the instructional program was running, but not necessarily that they learned the material from (or entirely from) the program. Once again, limitations of this design make it most useful for internal purposes, where results can be triangulated with other data to gain confidence that the ML instruction was responsible for the growth in skills. Educators can assess whether they are satisfied with both skill growth and attainment, and if not, consider adjusting future offerings of the ML program.

Comparison Group Design

The next incremental step in this progression of evaluation designs is to include a comparison group that does not experience the program between the administration of the pretest and posttest. Ideally, the comparison group is very similar to the treatment group. This is best done contemporaneously; the treatment group receiving the ML instruction and the comparison group that does *not* receive the instruction both take the pretest and posttests on the same schedule. This avoids capturing any other time-dependent changes that might affect the scores of one group and not the other. For example, if the control group was from a prior year and curricu-

---

[1] As the ML assessment landscape expands, a broad suite of grade-level assessments or adaptive tests may enable the pretest and posttest content to vary by grade (i.e., a seventh-grade test as a pretest and an eighth-grade test as a posttest) while still producing scores on a single developmental scale. Such assessment systems are relatively common in widely assessed subject areas, such as mathematics and literacy.

lum changes (other than starting the ML program) were instituted between the two years, those curriculum changes could be responsible for some or all of the learning captured for the treatment group.

In this design, a measure of the effect of the program can be obtained by first calculating average growth in each group and then subtracting the comparison group's growth from the treatment group's growth. A positive result provides evidence of an effect of the ML instructional program; on average, students in the program learned more ML material than the comparison group while the instructional program was running.

Weaknesses of this design include the risk that the treatment and comparison groups differ in unmeasured ways (in any way that is not measured by the pretest) and those differences affect their learning of ML skills between the pretest and posttest. This would cause the calculated estimate of the program effect to be biased. Moreover, differences in teacher effectiveness between the treatment and control groups can also bias the estimated program effect. The appendix discusses methodological enhancements that can mitigate, though not eliminate, these biases. With those enhancements, the quasi-experimental evidence generated by this design can be useful not only for internal purposes, but more broadly. The design can meet What Works Clearinghouse standards with reservation (Institute of Education Sciences, 2020), and the moderate or promising levels of evidence under ESSA (U.S. Department of Education, 2016). This means the results can provide a basis for other schools and districts to adopt the ML program with some confidence that it may be effective, and their implementations may be eligible for support under certain funding programs that require the use of materials that meet ESSA evidence standards.

Randomized Controlled Trial Design

The next increment brings us to the strongest available evaluation design—a randomized controlled trial. In this design, study participants are identified before deciding which of them will experience the ML instructional program. A random process is used to assign identified participants (ideally, both teachers and students) to a treatment group that undertakes the program or a control group that does not. At the time of randomization, the two groups are expected to have the same measured and unmeasured characteristics. For example, families may have influence over student development of ML skills, and this design helps to ensure that both experimental groups will be similar on that factor without having to measure it. This means that even a pretest is unnecessary because the two groups are expected to perform the same on this baseline measure, although reasons for retaining a pretest are discussed in the appendix.

Basic analysis can be performed just like in the comparison group design, by calculating the difference in growth between the treatment and control groups. Because even the pretest is expected to be equal in both groups, it can optionally be avoided, in which case the program effect is estimated by simply subtracting the control group average posttest from the treatment group average posttest.

The validity of this design to rigorously attribute student skill development to the ML program means that the evidence can be highly useful both internally and externally. The design can meet the highest tiers of evidence under both What Works Clearinghouse standards (i.e., without reservation (Institute of Education Sciences, 2020), and ESSA (i.e., strong evidence) (U.S. Department of Education, 2016). A downside of this design is that it requires the classes, teachers, or schools assigned to the control group to wait until the evaluation is finished before beginning implementation of the ML program. Doing this can interfere with teacher collaboration that could strengthen implementation.

How This Chapter Can Inform the Implementation and Evaluation of Media Literacy Educational Efforts

Any of the evaluation designs discussed here can be useful to those implementing ML educational efforts, as district decisionmakers, principals, instructional coaches, and teachers all have an interest in student learning. We recommend implementing the strongest design that is practical after careful consideration of the strengths and weaknesses of each. A strong evaluation design not only provides more-rigorous evidence for the educators who undertook the study, but also increases the utility of that evidence more broadly to other locales, particularly if the conditions and student populations are similar. However, small studies in specific populations may require further evaluation in other populations to produce more-generalizable evidence.

For implementors, a well-executed evaluation will go beyond examining average student outcomes to also examine variation in those outcomes. Such analysis may identify certain individuals or subgroups of students with performances that diverge from the average. Combining these data with information from implementation monitoring can help with interpretation; if the program appears to be more or less effective for certain students, implementation data may provide insights into the reasons. These insights might be actionable, suggesting ways to improve instruction or other aspects of implementation that could yield stronger program effects in the future.

Evaluators should think about summative evaluation when designing their project. To the extent possible, evaluation should be planned prospectively—a stronger research design, such as a randomized controlled trial, might be possible whereas it cannot be retrofitted to an implementation in progress. Statistical power is another important prospective consideration. Small studies may not yield statistically significant results, so conducting power calculations in advance may lead a more useful study. Experienced evaluators may be able to design studies to yield greater statistical power for a given sample size. For this and other reasons, it is useful to have a trained evaluator involved in the planning and execution of the evaluation. Districts or schools may have such expertise in house, but, if they do not, it may be worthwhile to engage an outside evaluator.

We have presented criteria for selecting an appropriate summative assessment for evaluation, and a variety of evaluation designs of increasing rigor. Even when the evaluation is for internal use—such as for school or district evaluators—it is advisable to use the best available summative measure and the strongest research design that is appropriate for the circumstances, to have the greatest confidence in the results. The most basic analyses for these designs can be easily performed without research training, and many evaluators can readily implement the enhancements discussed in the appendix.

CHAPTER EIGHT

Conclusion

Truth Decay permeates many aspects of life today, particularly the information ecosystem that people engage with on a daily basis. We view ML education as an important tool for mitigating Truth Decay for all ages and see a particularly strong opportunity to reach students in K–12 schools. Despite the promise of ML, we have identified some dimensions in which the field of ML education would benefit from greater attention. One of those areas is guidance for educators to support successful implementation of ML education, whether that be delivering explicit lessons or integrating concepts into core content areas. The second issue that would benefit from greater attention is the limited body of rigorous research that identifies what kinds of ML interventions work and under what conditions. Because of limitations like these, we do not have some of the tools we would have liked to offer in this report (e.g., providing an ML observation rubric in Chapter Six), because they do not yet exist.

Our implementation and evaluation framework addresses these challenges. The framework provides concise, step-by-step recommendations for undertaking ML interventions, implementing them thoughtfully, and studying their effects. The framework draws important connections between the world of education practice (implementation) and research (evaluation). Implementors, such as teachers, for instance, can use the framework to learn more about measuring student learning outcomes ways that are similar to how as a researcher would; evaluators can benefit from learning about the conditions influencing implementation of ML education (e.g., classroom, school, and environmental factors). Greater interaction between these often-separated groups can benefit both parties.

The chapters in our report follow the structure of the implementation and evaluation framework introduced in Chapter One. Each chapter focused on one of the six steps in that framework: (1) identifying ML learning expectations; (2) exploring conditions to support effective implementation; (3) selecting ML learning materials; (4) identifying measures of ML competencies; (5) monitoring interim progress; and (6) measuring summative outcomes. Each chapter highlights how the step might be useful to those who implement ML educational efforts and to those who evaluate the implementation and outcomes of those interventions. We summarize highlights from those chapters in the paragraphs to follow.

In Chapter Two, we introduced the Truth Decay ML standards, drawing from existing standards in ML, information literacy, digital literacy, and other related subject areas. Implementors can adopt or adapt these standards to set ML learning expectations for their students and inform their instructional decisionmaking. These learning expectations should guide the remaining steps in the implementation process, including selecting instructional resources and measures of student learning. Evaluators can use the standards to confirm alignment between learning expectations and the adopted curriculum and should seek similar alignment to a summative assessment for estimating effects of the ML program.

Next, in Chapter Three, we identified classroom, school, district and broader factors that can affect the success with which ML initiatives are implemented. In that chapter we provided a set of planning considerations that can be used as guidance for those implementing ML and highlighted some focal points that evaluators can reference when planning their data collection activities.

In Chapter Four, we outlined a typology of resources. There are myriad ML resources available, many free and accessible online, but little guidance about how to select resources that fit the particular needs of a specific classroom or school. ML instructional resources can vary along our seven dimensions, including whether the program is designed to be implemented as independent lessons or integrated into existing classroom instruction, and whether the resource focuses on teacher training. Importantly, we also highlighted the crucial dimension of accessibility. Viewing a resource along these dimensions can assist district leaders, principals, instructional coaches, and teachers in choosing instructional materials that are best suited to their contexts and help guide their adaptations of those materials to make the resource better fit their students' needs. Importantly, we highlight dimensions in which research indicates there is a clearly preferable choice—for instance, longer-term instruction is more effective than one-time instruction—so that implementors can weigh that against their own needs and constraints. The typology can also be useful for evaluators making decisions about how to study an intervention; for instance, a resource that requires a high degree of teacher mediation might suggest interviewing teachers for information about implementation, while a resource that students access online in their homes outside school hours might not.

We then discussed measurement considerations in Chapter Five, outlining different kinds of assessments available and their benefits and drawbacks. This included a discussion of alignment to the chosen learning objectives (e.g., the ML standards) and various other technical factors. Implementors can refer to this chapter to select appropriate FAs that will help them to adjust instruction and inform students of their progress. Evaluators may return to this chapter for information about selecting summative assessments that best measure the learning objectives.

In Chapter Six, we turned to monitoring implementation of the ML program. This chapter outlined several approaches to collecting qualitative data on implementation, from interviews to document collection. Implementors can monitor implementation using FA of student learning, gathering input about student experiences, and considering other factors that may interact with implementation. Evaluators should consider pairing any outcomes data with the kinds of qualitative implementation data discussed in this chapter; this is true for two primary reasons: First, evaluators can use these data to paint a descriptive picture of implementation, and second, the implementation information can help when interpreting quantitative results on program effects. For instance, implementation data can help surface common conditions across classrooms where student learning was greater than in other classrooms.

In Chapter Seven, we outlined considerations for summative evaluation. We discussed how to ascertain the impact of ML instruction on student skills, presenting a series of four progressively more-rigorous designs and discussing strengths and weaknesses of each. We also discussed the generalizability of evidence that results from these approaches; for instance, we suggest examining not just average outcomes, but variations that can be viewed alongside implementation data to seek insights into how the program can be improved. Basic analyses are presented that do not require specialized evaluation expertise. To the extent that districts or schools have access to trained evaluators, an appendix provides more-technical considerations that can enhance these analyses.

The implementation and evaluation framework should be a starting point for those implementing ML education—such as district decisionmakers, principals, instructional coaches, and teachers—and for those evaluating the impacts of ML educational interventions. As a next step, we hope to see implementors bringing this framework to their own planning and instruction, and, ideally, ML education being implemented more broadly across the United States. Teachers can use this at a classroom level, but the urgency of Truth Decay dictates that we consider implementation at the schoolwide, district, state, and even national levels. Given the limitations of current research, evaluators should use this framework to continue building the evidence base related to ML implementation and effectiveness. Moving forward, we encourage greater dialogue between these two portions of our audience—implementors and evaluators—as we suggested throughout by highlighting the interconnectedness of their work in each chapter. We encourage deeper reading and exploration into the topics covered in each chapter, with the hope that continued attention from both practitioners and researchers will address the ongoing and evolving challenge of Truth Decay.

APPENDIX

Enhancements to Evaluation Designs Discussed in Chapter Seven

In this appendix, we describe some basic methodological or analytic enhancements and contingencies related to the evaluation designs discussed in Chapter Seven and cite literature where these matters are discussed in greater detail.

The comparison group design and randomized controlled trial produce estimates of the effect of the ML program, although there are a variety of pitfalls that can arise in very small studies or if teachers of the treatment and comparison/control groups differ systematically (e.g., one holds inexperienced teachers and the other holds experienced teachers) (Institute of Education Sciences, 2020, p. 86).

When analyzed as described in Chapter Seven, a test of whether the result is statistically significant is not generated. A determination of statistical significance can be accomplished in a variety of ways; we suggest a linear regression because it can be extended to add features to the analysis. The regression can be as simple as specifying the outcome for each individual as the dependent variable (their posttest if no pretest was administered, or their growth score if a pretest was administered), and a treatment indicator as the independent variable—equal to 1 if the individual is in the treatment group or 0 otherwise. In the regression output, the coefficient on the treatment indicator is the estimated program effect and the standard error and statistical significance of that value are also reported.

Where a pretest is administered, slightly greater statistical power may be possible by using the posttest (rather than the growth score) as the outcome and including the pretest as a covariate. Another advantage of departing from the gain score approach is that the pretest and posttest then do not have to produce scores on the same scale. If additional student-level variables are available, such as other test scores and demographic information, these can also be added as covariates to increase statistical precision. The estimated effect, standard error, and test of significance remain those reported for the treatment indicator in regression output.

The availability of student background characteristics also enables the evaluator to calculate whether effects vary for different subgroups of students. This is generally accomplished by interacting the background variable (e.g., an indicator of poverty) with the treatment indicator.

Adjusting for covariates is particularly important in the comparison group design because it can help to diminish selection bias that results from differences between the treatment and comparison group. But even a robust set of covariates cannot eliminate the possibility of selection bias in the comparison group design. The analyst can further attempt to reduce this bias, while still not eliminating it, by applying matching or propensity score weighting in the comparison group design; the details of those methods are beyond the scope of this report (McCaffrey, Ridgeway, and Morral, 2004).

The standard errors and statistical tests produced by linear regression and many other methods are inaccurate when whole groups (classes or schools) are assigned to the treatment or control groups. This can be addressed by calculating cluster-robust standard errors, and—because the number of groups is likely to be small—using methods that function well in those circumstances. (Pustejovsky and Tipton, 2016).

Finally, the results of the above analyses all are on the scale of the test. If a program effect is estimated to be 5, the treatment group is estimated to score 5 points higher on the posttest. This may be a useful metric if the posttest scale is meaningful but not directly comparable to an evaluation that used a different test. For this reason, researchers standardize the program effect estimate by dividing by the standard deviation of the outcome (Hedges, 1981). This puts results from different studies onto a common scale; however, that scale can also be difficult to interpret, so evaluators may want to consider other ways to translate the results into more a interpretable metric (Baird and Pane, 2019).

Abbreviations

ESSA	Every Student Succeeds Act
FA	formative assessment
ML	media literacy
PD	professional development
SEL	social and emotional learning

References

Adams, William C., "Conducting Semi-Structured Interviews," in Kathryn E. Newcomer, Harry P. Hatry, and Joseph S. Wholey, *Handbook of Practical Program Evaluation*, Hoboken, N.J.: Wiley, 2015, pp. 492–505.

Allensworth, Elaine, and Holly Hart, "How Do Principals Influence Student Achievement?" University of Chicago Consortium on School Research, March 2018.

Allensworth, Elaine M., Camille A. Farrington, Molly F. Gordon, David W. Johnson, Kylie Klein, Bronwyn McDaniel, and Jenny Nagaoka, *Supporting Social, Emotional, & Academic Development*, Chicago: University of Chicago Consortium on School Research, October 2018.

American Educational Research Association, American Psychological Association, and National Council on Measurement in Education, *Standards for Educational and Psychological Testing*, Washington, D.C.: American Educational Research Association, 2014.

Antoniou, Panayiotis, and Mary James, "Exploring Formative Assessment in Primary School Classrooms: Developing a Framework of Actions and Strategies," *Educational Assessment, Evaluation and Accountability*, Vol. 26, No. 2, 2014, pp. 153–176.

Arizona Department of Education, Educational Technology Division, *State of Arizona Department of Education 2009 Educational Technology Standard*, Phoenix, Ariz., May 18, 2009.

Aronson, Brittany, and Judson Laughter, "The Theory and Practice of Culturally Relevant Education: A Synthesis of Research Across Content Areas," *Review of Educational Research*, Vol. 86, No. 1, March, 2016, pp. 163–206.

Atwater, Mary M., Melody Russell, and Malcolm Butler, eds., *Multicultural Science Education*, Secaucus, N.J.: Springer Science and Business Media, 2013.

Baird, Matthew D., and John F. Pane, "Translating Standardized Effects of Education Programs into More Interpretable Metrics," *Educational Researcher*, Vol. 48, No. 4, May 2019, pp. 217–228.

Baker, Garrett, Alice Huguet, Laura S. Hamilton, and John F. Pane, *Approaches and Obstacles to Promoting Media Literacy Education in U.S. Schools*, Santa Monica, Calif.: RAND Corporation, RR-A112-19, forthcoming.

Bennett, Randy Elliot, "Formative Assessment: A Critical Review," *Assessment in Education: Principles, Policy & Practice*, Vol. 18, No. 1, February 2011, pp. 5–25.

Best, Jane, and Allison Dunlap, *Continuous Improvement in Schools and Districts: Policy Considerations*, Denver, Colo.: McREL International, 2014.

Black, Paul, and Dylan Wiliam, "Developing the Theory of Formative Assessment," *Educational Assessment, Evaluation and Accountability*, Vol. 21, No. 5, January 23, 2009.

Blagg, Kristin, Erica Blom, Megan Gallagher, and Macy Rainer, *Mapping Student Needs During COVID-19*, Washington, D.C.: Urban Institute, April 29, 2020.

Bowen, Glenn A., "Document Analysis as a Qualitative Research Method," *Qualitative Research Journal*, Vol. 9, No. 2, August 3, 2009, pp. 27–40.

Bretschneider, Pamela J., Stefanie Cirilli, Tracey Jones, Shannon Lynch, and Natalie Ann Wilson, "Document Review as a Qualitative Research Data Collection Method for Teacher Research," *SAGE Research Methods Cases*, 2017.

Bronfenbrenner, Urie, *The Ecology of Human Development*, Cambridge, Mass.: Harvard University Press, 1981.

Bulger, Monica, and Patrick Davison, "The Promises, Challenges, and Futures of Media Literacy," *Journal of Media Literacy Education*, Vol. 10, No. 1, 2018, pp. 1–21.

Center for Media Literacy, "Media Literacy: A System for Learning Anytime, Anywhere: Part 1 Change Management," webpage, undated. As of June 21, 2021:
https://www.medialit.org/reading-room/media-literacy-system-learning-anytime-anywhere-part-1-change-management

Chang, I-Hua, "The Effect of Principals' Technological Leadership on Teachers' Technological Literacy and Teaching Effectiveness in Taiwanese Elementary Schools," *Educational Technology & Society*, Vol. 15, No. 2, 2012, pp. 328–340.

Chetty, Raj, John N. Friedman, and Jonah E. Rockoff, "Measuring the Impacts of Teachers II: Teacher Value-Added and Student Outcomes in Adulthood," *American Economic Review*, Vol. 104, No. 9, September, 2014, pp. 2633–2679.

Coburn, C. E., H. C. Hill, and J. P. Spillane, "Alignment and Accountability in Policy Design and Implementation: The Common Core State Standards and Implementation Research," *Educational Researcher*, Vol. 45, No. 4, 2016, pp. 243–251.

Collaborative for Academic, Social, and Emotional Learning, "District Theory of Action: Standards," webpage, undated. As of June 21, 2021:
https://casel.org/in-the-district/standards/

Common Sense Education, "Digital Citizenship Curriculum," webpage, undated. As of June 21, 2021:
https://www.commonsense.org/education/digital-citizenship/curriculum

Cooper Moore, David, and Theresa Redmond, "Media at the Core: How Media Literacy Strategies Strengthen Teaching with Common Core," *Voices from the Middle*, Vol. 21, No. 4, May 2014, pp. 10–15.

Crist, Courtney A., Susan E. Duncan, and Laurie M. Bianchi, "Incorporation of Cross-Disciplinary Teaching and a Wiki Research Project to Engage Undergraduate Students' to Develop Information Literacy, Critical Thinking, and Communication Skills," *Journal of Food Science Education*, Vol. 16, No. 3, July 11, 2017, pp. 81–91.

Critical Media Project, "DIY Activities," webpage, undated. As of June 21, 2021:
https://criticalmediaproject.org/diy-activities/

Darling-Hammond, Linda, Maria E. Hyler, and Madelyn Gardner, *Effective Teacher Professional Development*, Palo Alto, Calif.: Learning Policy Institute, June 5, 2017.

Datnow, Amanda, and Lea Hubbard, "Teacher Capacity for and Beliefs About Data-Driven Decision Making: A Literature Review of International Research," *Journal of Educational Change*, Vol. 17, No. 1, February 2016, pp. 7–28.

Datnow, Amanda, Brianna Kennedy-Lewis, and Vicki Park, "Affordances and Constraints in the Context of Teacher Collaboration for the Purpose of Data Use," *Journal of Educational Administration*, Vol. 51, No. 3, May 3, 2013, pp. 341–362.

Daugherty, Lindsay, Rafiq Dossani, Erin-Elizabeth Johnson, and Mustafa Oguz, *Using Early Childhood Education to Bridge the Digital Divide*, Santa Monica, Calif.: RAND Corporation, PE-119-PNC, 2014.

Davis, E. A., and J. S. Krajcik, "Designing Educative Curriculum Materials to Promote Teacher Learning, *Educational Researcher*, Vol. 34, No. 3, 2005, pp. 3–14.

Deal, Debby, Stephanie Flores-Koulish, and James Sears, "Media Literacy Teacher Talk: Interpretation, Value, and Implementation," *Journal of Media Literacy Education*, Vol. 1, No. 2, 2010, pp. 121–131.

Demski, Denise, and Kathrin Racherbäumer, "Principals' Evidence-Based Practice: Findings from German Schools," *International Journal of Educational Management*, Vol. 29, No. 6, August 10, 2015, pp. 735–748.

Durand, F. T., H. A. Lawson, K. C. Wilcox, and K. S. Schiller, "The Role of District Office Leaders in the Adoption and Implementation of the Common Core State Standards in Elementary Schools," *Educational Administration Quarterly*, Vol. 52, No. 1, 2016, pp. 45–74.

Dusenbury, Linda, Nick Yoder, Caitlin Dermody, and Roger Weissberg, "An Examination of K-12 SEL Learning Competencies/Standards in 18 States," CASEL Collaborating States Initiative, March 2020.

Eickelmann, Birgit, "Supportive and Hindering Factors to a Sustainable Implementation of ICT in Schools," *Journal for Educational Research Online*, Vol. 3, No. 1, 2011, pp. 75–103.

"Fact Check: No Evidence to Support QAnon Claims of Mass Arrests, Military Takeover, Illegitimacy of Biden's Presidency or Trump's Return to Power," Reuters, January 22, 2021.

Farrell, Caitlin C., and Julie A. Marsh, "Contributing Conditions: A Qualitative Comparative Analysis of Teachers' Instructional Responses to Data," *Teaching and Teacher Education: An International Journal of Research and Studies*, Vol. 60, No. 1, November 2016, pp. 398–412.

Fingar, Kathryn R., and Tessa Jolls, "Evaluation of a School-Based Violence Prevention Media Literacy Curriculum," *Injury Prevention*, Vol. 20, No. 3, June 2014, pp. 183–190.

Garrett, H. James, Mardi Schmeichel, Joseph McAnulty, and Sonia Janis, "Teaching and Learning News Media in Politically Unsettled Times," *Pedagogies: An International Journal*, Vol. 16, No. 1, March 16, 2020, pp. 44–61.

Guest, Greg, Emily Namey, Jamilah Taylor, Natalie Eley, and Kevin McKenna, "Comparing Focus Groups and Individual Interviews: Findings from a Randomized Study," *International Journal of Social Research Methodology*, Vol. 20, No. 6, February 13, 2017, pp. 693–708.

Hamilton, Laura, Richard Halverson, Sharnell S. Jackson, Ellen Mandinach, Jonathan A. Supovitz, Jeffrey C. Wayman, Cassandra Pickens, Emily Sama Martin, and Jennifer L. Steele, *Using Student Achievement Data to Support Instructional Decision Making*, Washington, D.C.: National Center for Education Evaluation and Regional Assistance, Institute of Education Sciences, U.S. Department of Education, NCEE 2009-4067, September 2009.

Hamilton, Laura S., Julia H. Kaufman, and Lynn Hu, *Media Use and Literacy in Schools: Civic Development in the Era of Truth Decay*, Santa Monica, Calif.: RAND Corporation, RR-A112-2, 2020a. As of June 22, 2021: https://www.rand.org/pubs/research_reports/RRA112-2.html

Hamilton, Laura S., Julia H. Kaufman, and Lynn Hu, *Preparing Children and Youth for Civic Life in the Era of Truth Decay: Insights from the American Teacher Panel*, Santa Monica, Calif.: RAND Corporation, RR-A112-6, 2020b. As of June 22, 2021: https://www.rand.org/pubs/research_reports/RRA112-6.html

Hamilton, Laura S., Brian M. Stecher, and Kun Yuan, "Standards-Based Accountability in the United States," *Education Inquiry*, Vol. 3, No. 2, June 2012, pp. 149–170.

Hansen, Michael, Elizabeth Mann Levesque, Jon Valant, and Diana Quintero, *The 2018 Brown Center Report on American Education*, Washington, D.C.: Brookings Institution, 2018.

Harrell, Margaret C., and Melissa A. Bradley, *Data Collection Methods: Semi-Structured Interviews and Focus Groups*, Santa Monica, Calif.: RAND Corporation, TR-718-USG, 2009. As of June 21, 2021: https://www.rand.org/pubs/technical_reports/TR718.html

Hedges, Larry V., "Distribution Theory for Glass's Estimator of Effect Size and Related Estimators," *Journal of Educational Statistics*, Vol. 6, No. 2, Summer 1981, pp. 107–128.

Hobbs, Renee, and Richard Frost, "Measuring the Acquisition of Media-Literacy Skills," *Reading Research Quarterly*, Vol. 38, No. 3, July–September 2003, pp. 330–355.

Hobbs, Renee, and Julie Coiro, "Design Features of a Professional Development Program in Digital Literacy," *Journal of Adolescent & Adult Literacy*, Vol. 62, No. 4, January 2019, pp. 401–409.

Hough, Heather, Demetra Kalogrides, and Susanna Loeb, *Using Surveys of Students' Social-Emotional Learning and School Climate for Accountability and Continuous Improvement*, Stanford, Calif.: Policy Analysis for California Education, March 2017.

Hubbard, Bibb, "Developing Life Skills in Children: A Road Map for Communicating with Parents," *Journal of Higher Education Theory and Practice*, Vol. 19, No. 3, 2019, pp. 33–54.

Huguet, Alice, Garrett Baker, Laura S. Hamilton, and John F. Pane, *Media Literacy Standards to Counter Truth Decay*, Santa Monica, Calif.: RAND Corporation, RR-A112-12, 2021. As of July 21, 2021: https://www.rand.org/pubs/research_reports/RRA112-12.html

Huguet, Alice, Jennifer Kavanagh, Garrett Baker, and Marjory S. Blumenthal, *Exploring Media Literacy Education as a Tool for Mitigating Truth Decay*, Santa Monica, Calif.: RAND Corporation, RR-3050-RC, 2019. As of June 22, 2021: https://www.rand.org/pubs/research_reports/RR3050.html

Huguet, Alice, Julie A. Marsh, and Caitlin C. Farrell, "Building Teachers' Data-Use Capacity: Insights from Strong and Developing Coaches," *Education Policy Analysis Archives*, Vol. 22, No. 52, July 23, 2014.

Humphrey, Neil, Alexandra Barlow, and Ann Lendrum, "Quality Matters: Implementation Moderates Student Outcomes in the PATHS Curriculum," *Prevention Science*, Vol. 19, February 2018, pp. 197–208.

Iachini, A. L., Beets, M. W., Ball, A., and M. Lohman, "Process Evaluation of 'Girls on the Run': Exploring Implementation in a Physical Activity-Based Positive Youth Development Program," *Evaluation and Program Planning*, Vol. 46, 2014, pp. 1–9.

Institute of Education Sciences, *What Works Clearinghouse: Standards Handbook Version 4.0*, Washington, D.C.: U.S. Department of Education, 2020.

International Society for Technology in Education, "ISTE Essential Conditions," webpage, undated. As of June 21, 2021: https://www.iste.org/standards/essential-conditions

Iowa CORE, "Best Practices in Social Studies Rubric," Des Moines: Iowa Department of Education, 2018.

Jeong, Se-Hoon, Hyunyi Cho, and Yoori Hwang, "Media Literacy Interventions: A Meta-Analytic Review," *Journal of Communication*, Vol. 62, No. 3, July 18, 2012, pp. 454–472.

Jimerson, Jo Beth, "Thinking About Data: Exploring the Development of Mental Models for 'Data Use' Among Teachers and School Leaders," *Studies in Educational Evaluation*, Vol. 42, 2014, pp. 5–14.

Jimerson, Jo Beth, and Jeffrey C. Wayman, "Professional Learning for Using Data: Examining Teacher Needs and Supports," *Teachers College Record*, Vol. 117, No. 4, 2015, pp. 1–36.

Jones, Stephanie M., and Jennifer Kahn, *The Evidence Base for How We Learn: Supporting Students' Social, Emotional, and Academic Development*, Washington, D.C.: The Aspen Institute, September 13, 2017.

Kavanagh, Jennifer, and Michael D. Rich, *Truth Decay: An Initial Exploration of the Diminishing Role of Facts and Analysis in American Public Life*, Santa Monica, Calif.: RAND Corporation, RR-2314-RC, 2018. As of August 2, 2020: https://www.rand.org/pubs/research_reports/RR2314.html

Literat, Ioana, "Measuring New Media Literacies: Towards the Development of a Comprehensive Assessment Tool," *Journal of Media Literacy Education*, Vol. 6, No. 1, 2014.

Livingstone, Sonia, and Ellen Helsper, "Gradations in Digital Inclusion: Children, Young People and the Digital Divide," *New Media & Society*, Vol. 9, No. 4, August 2007, pp. 671–696.

Lorenz, Ramona, Birgit Eickelmann, and Julia Gerick, "What Affects Students' Computer and Information Literacy Around the World? An Analysis of School and Teacher Factors in High Performing Countries," paper presented at Society for Information Technology & Teacher Education International Conference, Las Vegas, Nev., Association for the Advancement of Computing in Education, March 2, 2015.

Mahoney, Kerrigan, and Tehmina Khwaja, "Living and Leading in a Digital Age: A Narrative Study of the Attitudes and Perceptions of School Leaders About Media Literacy," *Journal of Media Literacy Education*, Vol. 8, No. 2, 2016, pp. 77–98.

Marsh, Julie A., and Caitlin C. Farrell, "How Leaders Can Support Teachers with Data-Driven Decision Making: A Framework for Understanding Capacity Building," *Educational Management Administration & Leadership*, Vol. 43, No. 2, August 18, 2015, pp. 269–289.

Marsh, Julie A., John F. Pane, and Laura S. Hamilton, *Making Sense of Data-Driven Decision Making in Education: Evidence from Recent RAND Research*, Santa Monica, Calif.: RAND Corporation, OP-170-EDU, 2006. As of June 15, 2021:
https://www.rand.org/pubs/occasional_papers/OP170.html

McCaffrey, Daniel F., Greg Ridgeway, and Andrew R. Morral, "Propensity Score Estimation with Boosted Regression for Evaluating Causal Effects in Observational Studies," *Psychological Methods*, Vol. 9, No. 4, December 2004, pp. 403–425.

McGrew, Sarah, Joel Breakstone, Teresa Ortega, Mark Smith, and Sam Wineburg, "Can Students Evaluate Online Sources? Learning from Assessments of Civic Online Reasoning," *Theory & Research in Social Education*, Vol. 46, No. 2, 2018, pp. 165–193.

McGrew, Sarah, Mark Smith, Joel Breakstone, Teresa Ortega, and Sam Wineburg, "Improving University Students' Web Savvy: An Intervention Study," *British Journal of Educational Psychology*, Vol. 89, No. 3, April 16, 2019, pp. 485–500.

Media Literacy Now, *U.S. Media Literacy Policy Report 2020: A State-by-State Survey of the Status of Media Literacy Education Laws for K-12 Schools*, Boston, January 2020.

Media Literacy Week, "National Media Literacy Alliance Joint Statement on Media Literacy Education," press release, October 2020.

Media Smarts, "Reality Check: The Game," webpage, undated. As of June 21, 2021:
https://mediasmarts.ca/digital-media-literacy/educational-games/reality-check-game

Meehan, Jessica, Brandi Ray, Amanda Walker, Sunny Wells, and Gretchen Schwarz, "Media Literacy in Teacher Education: A Good Fit Across the Curriculum," *Journal of Media Literacy Education*, Vol. 7, No. 2, October 2015, pp. 81–86.

Merriam, Sharan B., and Elizabeth J. Tisdell, *Qualitative Research: A Guide to Design and Implementation*, San Francisco, Calif.: John Wiley & Sons, 2015.

National Association for Media Literacy Education, "International Research Initiative," webpage, undated-a. As of July 9, 2021: http://18.232.142.12/research/international-research-initiative/

———, "Media Literacy, Defined," webpage, undated-b. As of September 16, 2020: https://namle.net/publications/media-literacy-definitions/

National Commission on Social, Emotional, and Academic Development, *From a Nation at Risk to a Nation at Hope: Recommendations from the National Commission on Social, Emotional, and Academic Development*, Washington, D.C.: Aspen Institute, 2019.

NewseumEd, homepage, undated. As of June 21, 2021: https://newseumed.org/

O'Connor, Edward P., and Elizabeth Witter Freeman, "District-Level Considerations in Supporting and Sustaining RtI Implementation," *Psychology in the Schools*, Vol. 49, No. 3, 2012, pp. 297–310.

Oberle, E., C. E. Domitrovich, D. C. Meyers, and R. P. Weissberg, "Establishing Systemic Social and Emotional Learning Approaches in Schools: A Framework for Schoolwide Implementation," *Cambridge Journal of Education*, Vol. 46, No. 3, 2016, pp. 277–297.

Patton, M. Q., "Enhancing the Quality and Credibility of Qualitative Analysis," *Health Services Research*, Vol. 34, No. 5, Pt. 2, December 1999, pp. 1189–1208.

Ponto, Julie, "Understanding and Evaluating Survey Research," *Journal of the Advanced Practitioner in Oncology*, Vol. 6, No. 2, March–April 2015, pp. 168–171.

Project Look Sharp, "List of Curriculum Kits by Content," webpage, undated. As of June 21, 2021: https://www.projectlooksharp.org/?action=kits#

Pustejovsky, James E., and Elizabeth Tipton, "Small-Sample Methods for Cluster-Robust Variance Estimation and Hypothesis Testing in Fixed Effects Models," *Journal of Business & Economic Statistics*, Vol. 36, No. 4, September 2016, pp. 672–683.

Schmeichel, Mardi, Jim Garrett, Rachel Ranschaert, Joseph McAnulty, Shannon Thompson, Sonia Janis, Christopher Clark, Stephanie Yagata, and Briana Bivens, "The Complexity of Learning to Teach News Media in Social Studies Education," *Journal of Media Literacy Education*, Vol. 10, No. 2, 2018, pp. 86–103.

Schwartz, Heather L., Laura S. Hamilton, Susannah Faxon-Mills, Celia J. Gomez, Alice Huguet, Lisa H. Jaycox, Jennifer T. Leschitz, Andrea Prado Tuma, Katie Tosh, Anamarie A. Whitaker, and Stephani L. Wrabel, *Early Lessons from Schools and Out-of-School Time Programs Implementing Social and Emotional Learning*, Santa Monica, Calif.: RAND Corporation, RR-A379-1, 2020. As of December 23, 2020: https://www.rand.org/pubs/research_reports/RRA379-1.html

Schweig, Jonathan, Laura S. Hamilton, and Garrett Baker, *School and Classroom Climate Measures: Considerations for Use by State and Local Education Leaders*, Creative Commons Attribution-NonCommercial 4.0 International License, RR-4259-FCIM, 2019. As of June 22, 2021: https://www.rand.org/pubs/research_reports/RR4259.html

Soland, Jim, Laura S. Hamilton, and Brian M. Stecher, *Measuring 21st Century Competencies: Guidance for Educators*, Santa Monica, Calif.: RAND Corporation, EP-50463, November 2013. As of August 1, 2020: https://www.rand.org/pubs/external_publications/EP50463.html

Stecher, Brian M., and Laura S. Hamilton, *Measuring Hard-to-Measure Student Competencies: A Research and Development Plan*, Santa Monica, Calif: RAND Corporation, RR-863-WFHF, 2014. As of August 1, 2020: https://www.rand.org/pubs/research_reports/RR863.html

Take Two Media Initiative, homepage, undated. As of June 21, 2021: https://www.taketwomediainitiative.org/

Tavlin, Noah, "How False News Can Spread," TED-Ed, video, undated. As of June 21, 2021: https://ed.ted.com/lessons/how-false-news-can-spread-noah-tavlin

Tucker, Eric, "U.S. Officials: Russia Behind Spread of Virus Disinformation," Associated Press, July 28, 2020.

Tully, Melissa, Emily K. Vraga, and Anne-Bennett Smithson, "News Media Literacy, Perceptions of Bias, and Interpretation of News," *Journalism*, Vol. 21, No. 2, October 11, 2018, pp. 209–226.

U. S. Department of Education, *Non-Regulatory Guidance: Using Evidence to Strengthen Education Investments*, Washington, D.C., September 16, 2016.

Van Gasse, Roos, Kristin Vanlommel, Jan Vanhoof, and Peter Van Petegem, "The Impact of Collaboration on Teachers' Individual Data Use," *School Effectiveness and School Improvement*, Vol. 28, No. 3, April 24, 2017, pp. 489–504.

Vinnakota, Raj, *From Civic Education to a Civic Learning Ecosystem: A Landscape Analysis*, Washington, D.C.: Education Writers Association, December 2019.

Vraga, Emily K., and Melissa Tully, "Media Literacy Messages and Hostile Media Perceptions: Processing of Nonpartisan Versus Partisan Political Information," *Mass Communication and Society*, Vol. 18, No. 4, April 22, 2015, pp. 422–448.

Vraga, Emily K., Melissa Tully, Heather Akin, and Hernando Rojas, "Modifying Perceptions of Hostility and Credibility of News Coverage of an Environmental Controversy Through Media Literacy," *Journalism*, Vol. 13, No. 7, August 30, 2012, pp. 942–959.

Wayman, Jeffrey C., Jo Beth Jimerson, and Vincent Cho, "Organizational Considerations in Establishing the Data-Informed District," *School Effectiveness and School Improvement*, Vol. 23, No. 2, 2012, pp. 159–178.

Webb, Theresa, and Kathryn Martin, "Evaluation of a U.S. School-Based Media Literacy Violence Prevention Curriculum on Changes in Knowledge and Critical Thinking Among Adolescents," *Journal of Children and Media*, Vol. 6, No. 4, 2012, pp. 430–449.

Weber, Christopher, *News Literacy Assessment*, Stony Brook, N. Y.: Center for News Literacy, Stony Brook University, 2012.

Wineburg, Sam, Joel Breakstone, Nadav Ziv, and Mark Smith, *Educating for Misunderstanding: How Approaches to Teaching Digital Literacy Make Students Susceptible to Scammers, Rogues, Bad Actors, and Hate Mongers*, Stanford, Calif.: Stanford History Education Group, Stanford University, Working Paper A-21322, 2020.